Dear Fran, Love Dulcie

Life and Death
in the
Hills and Hollows
of Bygone Australia

Collated by Victoria Twead

ANT PRESS

Len and Dulcie's Wedding, 10th July, 1954

 A catalogue record for this work is available from the National Library of Australia

NATIONAL LIBRARY OF AUSTRALIA

Photographs kindly donated by Fran Globke and the Clarke family

Published by Ant Press

Hardback ISBN: 978-1-922476-48-7

Paperback ISBN: 978-1-922476-47-0

Paperback Large Print ISBN: 978-1-922476-49-4

Hardback Large Print ISBN: 978-1-922476-50-0

Ebook ISBN: 978-1-922476-41-8

Each book purchased will help support Careflight, an Australian aero-medical charity that attends emergencies, however remote.

For Fran, who treasured and kept Dulcie's letters safe for more than 60 years.

For Terry and the Clarke family. Without their generosity this volume would never have existed.

For Bungundarra, Queensland, a land of hills and hollows where these events took place.

And finally, dedicated to the memory of brave young Dulcie Clarke, who will live forever through her letters to Fran.

CONTENTS

5th NOVEMBER 2020   1

PART I
1957 - 1962   9

PART II
1963 - 1968   71

PART III
1969 - 1973   131

PART IV
1974 - 1981   163

Epilogue   219
A request…   227
Acknowledgements   229
About Victoria Twead   231

The Old Fools series   233
Ant Press Books   237
Ant Press Online   241

5TH NOVEMBER 2020

Fran Globke

The following email appeared in my inbox, completely out of the blue, on 5th November 2020:

Dear Victoria,

Having enjoyed reading about your various life experiences in the past, I was eager to read "Two Old Fools Down Under". I was not disappointed. I enjoyed it thoroughly and see on Facebook you have also been traveling throughout Australia. This is one of the reasons I am writing to you now as Australia has played an important part of my life since the 1950s.

Through a United Nations "People to People Program", I began a penpal friendship with a young married girl in Queensland where she and her husband lived with their baby girl on a farm in the outback. I lived in Detroit, Michigan, a large city and was expecting my first child. And so our friendship started and we shared our lives by mail through the 1960s and '70s until her untimely death in 1981.

[Len, Dulcie and baby Karen, 1956]

The diversity of our lives showed our entirely different ways of life in two vastly different locales and we wrote of our daily lives sharing not only good times but our adventures, problems, and tragedies and our innermost thoughts. Her life presented daily challenges more worthy of any stories or TV series my sons could watch. We looked forward to her letters and I kept the letters in a scrapbook.

I wanted somehow to pay a tribute to her life and accomplishments by telling the story that chronicles her life from young girl to admirable Australian woman. But my husband and I began a new business and I kept putting it off. Periodically I would look at the scrapbook and think, *Someday, when I have time…*

Now I am 85 years old, with Parkinson's disease and my "someday" is, I'm afraid, coming too late. The desire to share Dulcie's life is still there. I re-read the letters and find they are most interesting to read, just as she wrote them. It is her story, I can't improve on that. But I don't know how to do this, and so I am writing to ask you if you could give me any advice as to what options I might have.

If you would like to read one of her letters—pick a month and year—and I will send you a copy of one close to that time. I cannot choose which one is more definitive of her, they are all most worthy of reading. Her life on the farm or ranch always was so different from mine. She faced many challenges, loved her land, and never gave up in the most trying of circumstances.

Thank you for taking the time to read my email, and thank you for sharing your adventures with all of us readers. What's next?

Fran Globkc
Coldwater
MI USA

"Joe!" I yelled from my office. "Listen to this!"

My husband joined me and listened quietly as I read Fran's email aloud.

"Lovely email," he said at last. "I would love to see a letter. Shall we ask Fran to send one?"

"I already have."

"Excellent."

The sample letter arrived and took our breath away. We told Fran we would be honoured to take over the project and publish the letters in book form. Fran agreed and provided us with all the letters. Joe set to work transcribing them.

But we wondered how Dulcie, an Australian girl, had been matched with Fran. I emailed Fran and received this reply:

Hello Vicky,

In 1957 I heard about the *People to People* program, the brainchild of President Dwight D. Eisenhower. He hoped it would encourage international friendships through a variety of activities including an exchange of letters.

I was intrigued. At 21, I had just had my first child and had left my job to be a full time wife and mother. I loved my new "career" but missed the city life I had also had.

I worked in the business hub of Detroit on the 21st floor of the National Bank Building as an Underwriter in an insurance firm. Our offices overlooked Windsor, Ontario, Canada across the Detroit River.

It was an hour's bus ride into the city from my home and an hour return in the evening. Downtown Detroit was at that time a thriving city with major shopping, theatres, museums, hotels, and led the automobile industry in the world.

When I heard of *People to People* it seemed like a wonderful way to contribute something to further understanding and peace, and I thought it'd be great to learn about places I probably would never see.

I sent in my information and I was given Dulcie's name in Australia. I also received information on another young woman in Tokyo, Japan. I excitedly answered both letters.

Unfortunately, my Japanese friend, who was a university student, lasted only two to three years because, after she graduated and began work in Tokyo, Asako found she couldn't keep up her English and so we decided to end our letters.

Her letters about her life, customs, and her experiences during the war were so different and I learned so much about Japanese culture. I treasure her letters also.

In Dulcie's letters I found another way of life which was so completely different from mine, and our friendship grew as we learned not only about our differences in lifestyle but also how much the same were our mutual fundamental beliefs on which we based our lives.

I am so glad I sent that first letter.

Fran

Other than a few tiny corrections and minor grammatical changes, the letters are all as we received them from Fran.

Occasionally Joe and I thought an explanation was necessary to clear possible ambiguities. These are few and appear within square brackets [thus]. For international readers we provided the approximate equivalent metric values for imperial weights and measures. We also converted Fahrenheit temperatures to degrees Celsius.

I believe Dulcie's letters are Australian historical treasures and I am eternally grateful to Fran and the Clarke family for allowing me to share them with the world.

Victoria Twead, 2021

PART I

1957 - 1962

3rd November 1957

Dear Fran,

Well, I was pleased to hear from you again and thank you very much for the photo. I have enclosed one of myself and Karen. As you can see she is not in a good mood. However she does have some sweet moments among the sour ones.

Well, the hot weather is with us now and the temperature goes to 115 degrees [46°C] almost every day. My garden has long since withered up and died, but it was beautiful while it lasted. I had balsams, petunias, zinnias, nasturtiums and a few other kinds.

Have you any household pets? We have three cats. Two tortoiseshell females and one black and white tomcat. Their names are Snuffy, Dotty, and Scotty. Karen loves them and is always carrying one around everywhere she goes. Of course we have numerous other animals on the farm, such as dogs, horses, cattle and pigs.

Well, now I had better answer some of the questions in your letter. I have already told you it can be very hot here, but no, it doesn't get very cold in winter. We don't have snow in Queensland

and the temperature only drops to between 20 and 30 degrees [C].

Our cars are both S.M. 1500s [Singer 1500] and are made in England. Cars are very expensive in Australia and there are lots and lots of people who cannot afford them. Also our roads are terrible things, just rough dirt tracks that are impossible to travel at much more than 30 miles per hour [50 kph]. In the cities they are made of bitumen. I shall be driving back to our farm shortly and although it is only a distance of approximately 500 miles [805 km], the roads are so bad, the journey usually takes two days.

Well, Fran, as news is short, I will close now and hope to hear from you again soon.

Yours sincerely,
Dulcie

29th November 1957 Mt. Ossa

Dear Fran,

I received your letter yesterday, so I am answering straight away, as we are leaving for home tomorrow. I will be really pleased to get back again and get the house and garden ready for Christmas.

Yes, I suppose you are excited about Ricky's first Christmas. This is Karen's second one, but as she was only 2 and ½ months old for the first one, this one we will really enjoy with her. Yes, she is walking, running too. She first walked at 12 months, but can't talk very much yet.

Well, yes, I have two brothers, Brian, 21, and Tom, 23, both single yet, no sisters. Len has two sisters, Violet 30, married with 3 children and Margaret, 20, single. No brothers. Both my people and Len's are farmers and are "next door neighbours", (the two farms join one another). Len's mother and father live apart and Margaret is on the farm with her mother, while his father works away. We very rarely see him.

My cat had 6 kittens last week. I killed four and kept two grey tomcats as my two other cats died from the heat a while back. Karen loves the kittens and when the mother cat gets out of the box, Karen gets in with the kits. They haven't got their eyes open yet, but when they have and are able to walk a bit she will have lots of fun with them.

My reading covers almost everything. I read anything I can get my hands on. But Pearl Buck is really one of my favourites. But Len and I both like war stories of the air-force or army. We have a large collection of books and have a library built in the new house. A few of my favourite war stories are "Down in the Drink", "The First and the Last" and we also have some written by German pilots in the last war, giving their side of the war. It is really interesting to read about both sides of the war. Two of these stories were "I Flew for the Führer" and "Stuka Pilot".

I am going to see about sending you a few Australian magazines. I won't be able to send them airmail, I don't think, but sent by ship they will probably take 2 or 3 months to reach you, however it won't matter if they are a bit old when you get them. You might still find them interesting. Do you have any weekly magazines for women over there?

Well, Fran, I had better close now and start on a bit of work. So hoping to hear from you soon.

Yours truly,
Dulcie

10th January 1958

Dear Fran,

Well, I was pleased to hear from you again, although I didn't really realise it had been so long since I last heard from you.

Time has seemed to take ages to go past this week and I've had no thoughts for anything other than Karen. She got out in the cow paddock a week or so ago and ate some poisonous berries and has been in a critical condition in the hospital since.

I can't get in to see her very often as the hospital is too far away. I did go in yesterday but she is unconscious and does not know me. When she had eaten them she started to take convulsions and choked. I took her with me in the car and raced for the doctor and although I travelled at 60 miles per hour [96 kph] nearly all the way, it seemed to take ages to get there.

Sometimes I wish we lived in the city, where we could have good roads and be close to all the amenities.

Yes, we have Christmas trees here, in fact I think Christmas is spent the same in nearly all parts of the world. Thank you very much for the greeting card you sent.

Yes, our family's birthdays all start to come now. First of all my brother Brian's is in February, mine is 21st of April and Tom's is in October.

I am having a 21st party this year. Mum and Dad say no one in our family has missed out on one yet and they don't see why I should either. But I'm not really looking forward to it.

My two little kittens are getting around now and are into all the mischief going.

Well, Fran, I had better close now and do some work.

So hoping to hear from you soon,

Dulcie

January 1958 Bungundarra, Yeppoon

Dear Fran,

Thank you very much for the snap of yourself, and Len with Ricky.

Ricky is a nice little chap. To look at the snap of him makes me wish Karen was a baby again. I would have another babe but the thought of going through all what I went through before puts me off it.

I was reading in an English magazine where in England and

America there are pain-killing drugs for childbirth, but here we just lie and wait till the babe is born and chew chewing-gum. I think I'll save up and go overseas to have my next one if the doctors are so good as I am led to believe.

It is very hot today. The temp is 110 [43°C] and we are only half-way through the day, so it will probably get hotter in the evening.

I am rounding up some more magazines to send to you. I haven't received yours yet.

The pineapple harvest is drawing to a close at last. We got approximately a hundred and fifty thousand from ours with just a few hundred more to come. It wasn't a bad season but we hope to do better next time. The next crop comes off in September.

Well, Fran, I must close now and get lunch ready.

So till next time,

Dulcie

10th February 1958

Dear Fran,

Well, yes, I do have good news about Karen this time.

She has had a few skin grafts on her feet but for the time being she is home with us. Her feet are the worst and the rest of her body looks just as if she was never hurt. I would have hated her to be disfigured. However, even her feet look good now. Thanks to the doctors and God, I am sure.

You must have been really excited when Ricky had his birthday. It was bad, your mother not being able to be there to celebrate too.

We have had some rain here at long last. We are right in the middle of summer here, so I expect you will be having winter over there.

I'm glad you liked the magazines. Would you like me to send you some more? Any particular ones? I am eagerly awaiting yours.

We are in full swing with the pineapple harvesting now. We send most of ours to the cannery to be canned and exported to England and other countries. They are very prickly things but really taste nice.

I am enclosing a few photos for you and I hope you can decipher what they are as they aren't very good. Do let me have some of your family as soon as you get some, won't you.

Well, I had better close now as its 4:30 and I haven't prepared tea [the evening meal] yet. So hoping to hear from you soon.

Yours truly,
Dulcie

—✳——✳——✳—

1st April 1958

Dear Fran,

Well, for the past week we have been having great deluges of rain. But today there has only been light showers so I guess it is starting to fine up. My garden and lawn welcomed the rain and everything looks lovely and fresh.

I have had a run of abscesses in my right ear and it is terrible sore. I have drops to put in it and two different kinds of tablets to take, but they don't seem to make much difference. However I suppose like everything else, they will have an ending.

Well, you are more correct, about the way pineapples grow, than Dick is. They grow on a spiky mass of prickly leaves about three to four feet [91 to 122 cm] high and they shoot out the fruit on a stem at the top. I have taken some photos to send you when they are printed.

Thank you for the magazines. I have read them from cover to cover. I am sending you another bundle with this letter.

The kittens are lovely and the mother cat is expecting again. She should have them any day now. We bought Karen a collie pup a couple of weeks ago and she just adores her. She is black and white and has long hair. We called her Muchadilla (Muchy for short) which means in Aboriginal, "Fat Doggy".

Well, Fran, I had better close for now and get some work done. So cheerio,

Dulcie

25th April 1958

Dear Fran,

Thank you ever so much for the lovely birthday card and good wishes. It arrived just an hour or so after the party had started.

We all had a lovely time at the party and after the feast was over we played games and danced for hours. Karen stayed up the whole time and really enjoyed herself. She didn't cry once, but she ate and ate and when we got home she was fast asleep in the car.

I received some wonderful presents, things that I hadn't dreamed anyone would ever give me. But next morning we had to get up and work again and that was the hardest part of it all.

We are coming into winter here now and it is chilly during the nights and in the mornings. You said in your letter when it was 70 degrees [21°C] you didn't need a coat when you're out.

But when the temp drops from 110 to 70 [43 to 21°C] here we are freezing. It was only 73 [23°C] this morning but we were all crowded around the heater trying to get warm and wrapped in coats. I think I'd die if I went over there during winter.

My garden looks lovely now. All the balsams are in bloom and the gladioli, sweet peas, stocks and phlox. The watsonias are growing up into buds also.

Well, it is 6 o'clock so I had better start preparing some supper.

So best wishes,
Dulcie
PS enclosed are some snaps of the pineapples and Karen.

21st May 1958

Dear Fran,

I've been hoping and praying to get a letter from you this past fortnight. I don't know which way to turn or what to do with myself.

Karen was drowned on Sunday 4th of May. She wandered away about 8 o'clock in the morning and when I went to find her at 9 o'clock she was nowhere to be seen. We searched everywhere and Len went about ½ mile away and found her drowned in an old well. She still had her pyjamas and slippers on. She was dead when I went to meet him after he called out. But we tried to revive her. I just couldn't believe she was gone. After a while we put her in the car and raced for a hospital. The police and a doctor met us on the road and they said they could do nothing for her. I still find it hard to believe she's gone and everything around the house reminds me of her.

Sometimes I feel like taking my own life but I know it would only make Len's grief heavier and would be a selfish thing to do.

Her pets miss her badly too and the dog keeps searching for her. If I get rid of her clothes, toys, furniture and pets, I might feel better. I just don't know what to do half the time.

Well, Fran, please write soon as I do look forward to your letters and I hope you and your family are all well and happy.

Love,
Dulcie

18th June 1958

Dear Fran,

Well, it is now 6 weeks since Karen's death, I don't feel too bad now but it is terribly lonely on my own all day. Len is working in the far paddocks now and takes his lunch with him. I don't know what to do with myself half the day.

We have a neighbour now. A man and his family bought the old farm next door to us but their house is about a mile away, so I don't get much opportunity to talk to them.

Winter has started here and the nights are getting very chilly. There is a carnival on in Rockhampton this week. Do you have carnivals or festivals over there? We might go up to Rockhampton one day to see it. I made myself a new suit to go in. It is made of nylon and wool mixture material in grey with small specks of yellow and red in it. It looks quite nice and has a fitted coat and pleated skirt.

Yes, Fran, I did get your magazines and have started to read them now. I am pleased to hear you got your boat motor back. It is terribly hard when you've saved to buy something and then some mean thing takes it.

My garden looks wonderful too. The sweet peas are in full bloom and are a variety of colours.

I hope you had a lovely night out on your wedding anniversary. Ours is not until 10th July and we will be 4 years married.

I believe you told me in a previous letter you were expecting another babe. Well, good luck to you and I expect you'd like a little girl for a mate for your boy.

We are starting to harvest the winter crop of pineapples now and during winter they are always very sour, as there isn't much sun to sweeten them up.

I went to Yeppoon yesterday and did my monthly shopping. I had quite a good time and met some friends I haven't seen for quite a while.

We will be able to have the telephone installed soon. The line is being brought this way slowly. At present we have a trip of 5 miles [8 km] to the nearest phone.

Well, Fran I guess I had better close as I hear our transport carrier coming to collect and deliver our weekly mail.

So Love,
Dulcie

15th July 1958 Bungundarra

Dear Fran,

Well, I've just had the most happiest shock. I'm nearly four months pregnant and I didn't know it! I knew my periods had ceased some months ago but I thought the shock of Karen's passing had done it. But yesterday I decided I'd go see my doctor about it and I almost fainted when he told me it was a baby. December 29th is my due date. But I'm not even an inch [2.5 cm] bigger than my normal measurements, so I still find it hard to believe.

Len and my wedding anniversary was on 10th July, but we both forgot it till 3 days later. I was doing some accounts and looked at the calendar and we both had a good laugh about it.

We are in mid-winter now but have only had 3 or 4 cold nights. We are still picking pines and Len is also planting more.

I went shooting a couple of days ago, with my dog. I had a good day out and got the dog a wallaby. Len and I are going again over the weekend. The wild-duck season is open now, so we are going to see if we can get some.

My garden is slowly going off now, with the cooler air. Nothing likes to grow in winter.

Well, Fran, I had better close now, so write soon.

Love,
Dulcie

16th August 1958

Dear Fran,

I haven't heard from you for quite awhile and I wondered if you were alright. I hope you or your family are not ill. It has been raining here for the past week and we have had just about enough now. My garden has soaked up all it can hold.

My young dog died last week from a shellback tick bite. I took her to the vet and had her given an injection and tablets but she died two days later, after becoming paralyzed. So my only house pets now are two cats.

I am listening to the Hit Parade as I write this. "Twilight Time" and "The Ballad of the Teenage Queen" are the two top numbers.

Well, Fran, excuse this short note and I hope you and your family are all well.

Yours truly,
Dulcie Clarke

29th August 1958

Dear Fran,

Well, I was pleased to hear from you again and thank you so much for the photo.

Your little boy [Ricky] is a lovely little fellow and looks like his father a bit, doesn't he?

I think I must be going to have a boy this time as it moves and kicks too much for a girl. I really would like a little girl though.

I have gained one pound and have made a blue and pink poplin maternity suit but I don't need to wear it yet. The baby must be terribly small.

I am eating all I can in the hopes that it will make him larger.

A wallaby is a smaller edition of a kangaroo. It only grows about 2 feet [61 cm] high (standing on its hoppers) and hops along the same as a kangaroo. I have enclosed a snap of a pet one I had.

It grew up and "Went Bush". They are grey in colour and eat grass.

I have to drive into Yeppoon tomorrow and am not looking forward to the trip one bit. The road is rough and dusty and it takes ¾ of an hour to go 13 miles [21 km]. I wish we owned an aeroplane.

I have two parrots nesting in a bloodwood tree near the house. The female bird is sitting on some eggs.

Well, Fran, I will have to dash and start supper as the time is 6 o'clock and Len will be in soon.

So love from,
Dulcie

—✳——✳——✳—

10th October 1958

Dear Fran,

I am so sorry to hear you have been ill and hope you are quite better now. We must have caught the infection from one another as I too have been ill for two weeks with influenza. I had a terrific cough for eight days and lost three pounds [1.4 kg] in weight.

However I am okay now and have been doing some gardening today. It is a showery day and very good for transplanting things. I have a lovely lot of watermelons that should be ripe about December. Also my watsonias are in full bloom, and they are really beautiful.

Len bought me another little pup last week. He is just a blue and white cattle dog with a white tip on his tail, so I call him "Tip". He is only as big as a kitten but so fat he can hardly turn around.

How did you get on with your house hunting? Have you found one suitable? You ask if many people own aeroplanes for private use here. Well, in Western Queensland, on most of the sheep and cattle stations, they have aeroplanes instead of cars as there are no roads to travel on. They are only two to four passenger Austin aircrafts.

My stamp collection has just about got beyond me so I think I'll sell it if I can. The album is fairly valuable now and I should make a good profit. I'll get some together for you to give the boy you say collects them.

It doesn't matter if they are postmarked lightly, but of course they wouldn't be so valuable as the unmarked ones. However, I don't think a child would mind as long as they were different to what the other children had.

Well, Fran, as it is nearly lunch time I had better close.

So love,

Dulcie

14th October 1958

Dear Fran,

Well, we've been having a hectic time here lately with the temp around 112 degrees [44°C] each day and bushfires have been terrific. Most of the other farmers around are burned right out and goodness knows what their cattle will eat. Also a lot of pineapples have been burned.

The worst pineapple fire was just a week ago. I was on my way home in the car from Yeppoon and I could see a terrific cloud of smoke rising. When I reached home I found Len had gone to help with it. So I went too. One family had to leave their home as the smoke was suffocating.

Two farms were being burnt and as the men were all away at the fire front, the women were in a panic. One woman has eight children and expecting another in two weeks time and the other has two little babies. I collected both the women and children in the car and made a dash out along the road, but we hadn't got far when we discovered we were hemmed in with fires cutting across the road. I turned back and parked the car in a piece of ploughed ground. We nearly all died from the smoke. The babies had a tough time.

Our house was partly burnt and on another farm fifteen thousand pineapples were completely destroyed. It is a terrible loss to the owner as they were all in fruit and would be ready to pick in December.

We had all our country burnt clean, but we saved the pines. Today the temp is 108 degrees [42°C] in the shade with a gale force wind blowing so I expect there will be more fire outbreaks today.

I like your names for the baby. I like Linda especially. I have gained seven pounds [3 kg]. You haven't got far to go to the hospital so you are very fortunate. It is reassuring to know one hasn't far to go isn't it? I have a trip of 2 and ½ hours from home. But I always have one car here so I can go if Len is away. I can always shorten the drive by a ½ hour if I need to go really fast.

Your house sounds like it will be nice and comfortable. You will be able to move in with the new babe.

Well, Fran, I had better close and get lunch started.

So love,

Dulcie

--×----×----×--

27th January 1959

Dear Fran,

So sorry to have been so long in answering your letter and congratulations on the birth of your son.

We, too, have a son and we named him Terrence Leonard Clarke. He was 9 pounds [4 kg] at birth and has dark hair and blue eyes. I just made it to the hospital in time. The water broke at home and by the time I'd driven to the hospital I had only an hour before his birth.

Labour started at 4 o'clock Tuesday evening and I was home on my own. I waited till 8 o'clock, thinking Len might be back from his trip, but then I thought I had better go so I got the car out and the drive took me three hours as I had to go slowly when the pains got bad. I arrived at the hospital at 11 and the baby was born about 11:45. So altogether labour lasted only about 8 hours.

It is very wet here and the roads are just quagmires. Len has to pull the truck-load of pines with the tractor, while I drive the truck. The mud is so deep that only part of the wheels are visible.

Terry sleeps on the seat while I'm working with Len. He is bottle fed and is quite a contented little fellow.

Well, Fran, I will have to close and get supper ready.

So love from,

Dulcie

1st March 1959

Dear Fran,

So pleased to hear from you and hope you and babe are doing well. Terry is doing good and is five weeks old and weighs 12 pounds [5.4 kg]. He has been eating cereal and fruit for three weeks now. I feed him on a cereal called Larese and he really loves it. He also has plenty of pineapple juice to drink.

How is your ankle? I hope it is doing well.

I hope the weather has warmed up for you. I would gladly send you some of our heat, if possible. The temp has been around 100 degrees [38°C] for the past month and the baby feels it too. He wears only a nappy [diaper] both day and night.

The heat has been terrific in the southern states. The temp there is usually only in the 60s [16°C] however, it has been around the century for a while and 30 babies have died so far and a number of elderly people also. We are used to the heat in Queensland and would probably die if we got a cold snap.

I'm sorry to hear you have to search for another home. However, it would be no good buying one and not being happy in it.

Yes, Fran, I will send you some more magazines when I go to Yeppoon next week or so. The mail transport only takes letters as he is unable to quote the amount of postage on parcels and papers, so we have to wait till we go to town.

We are still picking pineapples although the peak of the crop has finished. I have a number of abscesses on my arms and my feet from pineapple prickles. My blood is a bit out of order and the sores have turned to abscesses. Normally they don't bother me.

Well, Fran, I have to get the washing out so I will close for now.

Love,

Dulcie

1st April 1959

Dear Fran,

Well, you seemed very pleased in your last letter because the snow had gone. I hope you are still having lovely weather. It has been so hot here last week, over 100 degrees [38°C] all the time and one day it reached 112 degrees [44°C].

However we are having some rainy showers today and everything is starting to look green again.

The road from Yeppoon to here is being widened to 12 feet [4 metres] now. It was only 7 feet [2 metres] wide before and one had to drive into the trees if anyone wanted to pass.

They have a bulldozer pushing down trees and they are also blasting the big ones. It will be so much better but at present it's very boggy. We have no bitumen on it, only just a dirt road. Your new house sounds so lovely. I hope you are happy in it. It is a great upheaval to have to pack up and move.

Yes, it would be tough to start off in Alaska and as you say the nearest doctor is 100 miles [161 km] away, maybe they could adopt the Australian way of solving the problem. We have what is called a "Flying Doctor Service" to outback places where no doctors are available for up to 500 miles [805 km]. The doctor is paid by the government and given an aeroplane and pilot and flies to the places where he is needed. Most stations (cattle and sheep) have airfields and all have pedal wirelesses (or as I think they are called over there) two-way radios.

When the doctor is wanted they radio the doctor's radio and then he answers them and flies off to attend the cases or bring them to a hospital, depending on how serious they are.

Well, Mark sounds to be doing fine. Terry is 15 and ½ pounds [7 kg] now and also has hair about an inch [2.5 cm] long. He only had a fuzz when he was born.

Len is planting pineapples now, but I can't help him as it is much too cold and rainy to let Terry sleep out in the car while I work. So I have to stay at home. However, I might go tomorrow.

Well, Fran, I must close now and do some baking.

So love from,

Dulcie

29th April 1959

Dear Fran,

Thank you so much for the lovely card for my birthday, it was a pleasant surprise to know you had remembered.

Your memory must be much better than mine, for the date of your birthday has slipped from my memory. Could you please tell me next time you write when yours and Ricky's is?

Yes, Fran, the years do fly by as we are getting older. It is almost a year since we lost Karen, but it doesn't seem so long since she was toddling around the house. I still remember her very clearly, I wonder shall I ever forget?

We have just passed another Anzac Day also. Anzac means Australian New Zealand Army Corps and is a tribute to the men from both countries who fought side by side and died.

Men of both World Wars march through the streets and stand at the cenotaph while prayers are said and the names of the fallen from the district are read out. Wreathes are then laid, the last post sounded and two minutes silence observed.

A concert is held each Anzac Day, at night, and the proceeds go to charity. My eldest brother Tom and I are always among the artists performing.

Tom sang and played his guitar, doing "There's a Gold Mine in the Sky" and "Don't ever take the Ribbons from your Hair". I sang with piano accompaniment "Goodbye" from [the operetta] "The White Horse Inn" and "The Twelfth of Never".

We all had a wonderful time and thoroughly enjoyed ourselves.

We are coming into winter now. The nights have been cool, around 60 degrees [16°C] and the days are only about 80 to 85 [26 - 30°C]. I don't like winter much as I always seem to be cold. I have knitted Terry a couple of jumpers and one for Len and am now doing one for myself.

Len and I and my brother Brian went shooting last night with spotlights. I got 2 possums and then Len and Brian got a couple of kangaroos, wallabies and whiptails.

My rifle is too light for the larger animals. It is a Lithgow .22 and Len's is an American Service Mark II. Brian has a .303 and a Mauser complete with telescope, which enables him to see much further.

We poisoned all the animals with strychnine for dingo baits.

The dingos are bad now and are killing calves and poultry. They have also killed some dogs. They had a go at our dog a couple of nights ago but he was off his chain and ran up into the house.

Well, Fran, Terry has just woken up so I must bath and feed him.

So love from,

Dulcie

———✳——✳——✳——

29th May 1959

Dear Fran,

Well, I hope you are settled into your new home by now and are quite pleased with it.

We have been having some rain here for the last week and the roads are very boggy. I went into Yeppoon yesterday and had a hard time getting in and out of some creeks.

It is Len's birthday today. He is 31 years old.

I haven't heard any of the songs that are on your hit parade at present. They usually take a year or so to get out here. At present some of our top ones are "A fool such as I", "Smoke gets in your eyes", "I can't stop loving you", "Come in Stranger".

Terry is 4 months and 1 week now.

I heard on the radio yesterday that we might be going to get TV soon. The southern states all have it but Queensland is quite backward and doesn't have anything like they do.

Len and I love to read also, and have quite a large library. Our latest edition being "Commander Crabb".

Well, Fran, I must close now and do some work.

So love from,

Dulcie

———✳——✳——✳——

23rd June 1959

Dear Fran,

Thank you for the photos. Mark looks a lovely little fellow. That is a nice picture of your husband, you and the children.

Fran, Dick, Mark and Ricky Globke

It is nice to have family pictures, don't you think? Dad used to take a lot of pictures of my brothers and I as children. They are good to look back at now.

You certainly are having hot weather. I hope you had some rain to cool things off. It is raining here at present. We aren't having much of a winter this year. It rains nearly every week. My fowls don't like it and have gone off the lay.

Yes, Fran, "On the Beach" was filmed in Melbourne, in the state of Victoria. I haven't seen it yet but I would love to as I've never been to any of the other states. They are supposed to be very lovely and much ahead of Queensland.

I'm listening to the Hit Parade at present. "Personality" is on top. I think you told me it was one of your hits a while back. I like it too.

I went shooting last night. The dog saw a possum, but my spotlight couldn't pick it out of the leaves. It started to rain soon after, so I had to come home with nothing. The dog was very sad about it.

Well, Fran, I have to drive to the dentist's in a short time so I will close and post this then.

Love,
Dulcie

10th August 1959

Dear Fran,

Well, I hope Mark is much better now. I haven't heard of the sickness you said he had. I suppose it has a different name out here. I suppose the rash was very itchy and irritated the little fellow.

Terry has been a bit cranky lately. He has two little teeth just through the gum on the lower jaw.

Yes, Fran, I also have been very busy doing nothing. Len has been away for 3 weeks, only comes home on Saturdays, and during the week I have a job finding something to do.

I think I've read one of the books you mentioned, "Home before Dark". If it wasn't the same one, it was much the same, about a woman home from a mental institution. I will post you another bundle of magazines on the 11th August. I was given a copy of the American Saturday Evening Post and one called Life a few weeks ago. I liked them very much. I also like the Redbook you have sent a few times.

The sky is very cloudy today and looks like rain. I hope we get an inch or so. My garden could do with a good soaking. I have prepared a bed along the front fence for a dozen roses. I haven't got them in yet.

Well, Fran, I have some ironing to do so I guess I had better close now.

Love,
Dulcie

---✗———✗——✗---

10th October 1959

Dear Fran,

Well, I hope you enjoyed your Labour Day holiday. Your new boat sounds lovely.

We went fishing yesterday. We have to go about 320 miles [515 km] and when it rains it is a terrible road. Rain started 2 hours after we got there and coming back we got bogged in the salt pan. The salt pan is about 3 miles [5 km] across and as soon as we got out of one bog hole we went into another. Rain was falling all the time. Terry enjoyed himself in the car while Len and I were out digging the mud away.

Mark is a bit smarter than Terry. He can only stand up and walk if one holds his hands. He never learned to crawl much but loves to pull himself up on any piece of furniture. He has 6 teeth now. Last week he had his last injection for Tetanus, Diptheria and Whooping Cough. He still has to get them for smallpox and poliomyelitis.

I have to go into hospital for an operation on my ears. I hope I'm not in too long. I shall miss Terry. I'll bet he'll miss me too and probably play up a bit with his father.

My brother Tom and his wife have a baby daughter, Veronica Ann, 7 pounds 14 ounces [3.6 kg] at birth. Well, Fran, I had better close now and feed Terry.

Love from,
Dulcie

---✗———✗——✗---

5th January 1960

Dear Fran,

Well, what kind of Christmas did you have? We had a very quiet time as we were not able to go anywhere. Flood rains set in during Christmas week and most of the Queensland roads were blocked.

We had dinner with Dad and Mum and one brother. Terry loved the stocking hanging on his cot on Christmas morning and soon had everything out of it.

The rain has cleared up now and we are having very hot weather. The temp over the last 3 days has been up in the 100 degrees [38°C]. I am writing this letter at 12 noon and the temp is 109 [43°C].

Terry doesn't mind. He has a tub of water on the verandah and runs around in the nude and gets in and out of the water when he likes.

I am taking him to Rockhampton on the 20th (his birthday) to have his photograph taken. By the way, Fran, wish Mark a belated many happy returns from me and also to Ricky who will have a birthday by the time you get this letter.

We went to Rockhampton to watch my eldest brother race his Gnat last week. He won one race and during the second he collided with another Gnat and hit the safety fence and rolled over 4 times.

He wasn't hurt, only dazed. He is racing again on Saturday night.

I have lots of chickens out now and have to watch out for hawks during the day. They glide in and take the chicken before one can see them. I shot three last week.

Len went out New Year's night. I stayed home as we have been troubled by dingos.

During the night I heard a noise in the duck pen. I fired at a pair of eyes, thinking it was a dingo. When I went to look I found it was a wild black dog I'd shot.

We haven't lost any birds since so I think it must have been the dog taking the birds all the time.

Enclosed is a photo of both brothers ploughing. Tom driving a crawler and Brian on the Fordson [tractor].

Well, Fran, I must close now and see about lunch.

So love from,

Dulcie

10th February 1960

Dear Fran,

It is 11 a.m. and raining hard here at present. We are in the middle of our wet season and our roads are flooded and creeks are bonkers.

Our summer pineapple crop is just coming off and we are having trouble getting the fruit carted. We pick and pack the pines into crates and then they have to be carted on the truck 15 miles [24 km] to Yeppoon railway station.

They are then taken by train another 500 miles [805 km] to Northgate Cannery. We have one creek 3 miles [5 km] from here that rises over the bridge and cuts us off and then 6 miles [10 km] further on the other creek has a very old bridge over it.

[Dulcie's brother, Brian, leaning against a truck carrying pineapples, which has a flat tyre.]

That one can't carry more than 6 tons [6100 kg] over. Therefore we have to make a detour of about 18 miles [29 km] of more boggy roads.

Len is picking at present and after I finish getting lunch on to cook I shall have to join him. Terry is playing around in the living room.

Terry has quite recovered from the measles now and is quite happy again.

You asked about the translation of Waltzing Matilda, Fran, so I have written it on a sheet at the end of this letter. You also asked about the meaning of Bungundarra, Yeppoon.

Well, Bungundarra is the name of the farming settlement here and is an aboriginal word meaning "Hills and Hollows" which describes this area very well.

Yeppoon is 15 miles [24 km] away and is a small place consisting of railway station, school and post office with a few houses, etc. It is an English word I believe and there is also a town named Yeppoon in South Africa.

Yes, Fran, a Gnat is a small racing car. I will get a snap of Tom's and send it to you with the next letter.

I don't know if you sing Waltzing Matilda the same as we do but anyway I've written it the way we sing it. I hope you can fathom it out.

Thank you for the photo, Fran. Both little boys are very much alike I think.

Well, Fran, I must away and go pick pines.

So love to all,

Dulcie

Ricky and Mark Globke

Waltzing Matilda

Once a jolly swag-man, (meaning a kind of hobo) camped by a billabong, (Aboriginal for water hole)
Under the shade of a coolabah tree, (a soft-wood tree)
And he sang as he watched and waited till his billy boiled,
You'll come a-Waltzing Matilda with me. (Old swag men called their swags or blanket rolls Matilda or Bluey.)

Down came a jumbuck (sheep) to drink at the billabong,
Up jumped the swagman and grabbed him with glee, (meaning he
was hungry and was very pleased to see the sheep)
And he sang as he shoved that jumbuck in his tucker bag, (tucker
means food and swaggies carried a bag with their food in it.)
You'll come a-Waltzing Matilda with me.

Down came the squatter (a squatter is a man who owns land and
runs cattle or sheep. I think you call them ranch owners) mounted
on his thoroughbred, (riding a well-bred horse)
Down came the troopers (mounted police) one, two three,
"Where's that jolly jumbuck you've got in your tucker bag?
You'll come a-Waltzing Matilda with me." (They would take him
and gaol him for stealing the sheep.)

Up jumped the swagman and sprang into the billabong,
"You'll never take me alive," said he,
And his ghost may be heard as you pass by the billabong,
"You'll come a-Waltzing Matilda with me." (The swag-man
drowned himself rather than be gaoled and his ghost haunts the
waterhole.)

(A chorus is sung after every verse:)

Waltzing Matilda, Waltzing Matilda,
You'll come a Waltzing Matilda with me,
And he sang as he watched and waited till his billy boiled,
You'll come a-Waltzing Matilda with me.

9th March 1960

Dear Fran,
     I was so disappointed when I opened your last letter. The photos
you had enclosed were stuck together and when we parted them

most of the print came off. I am returning them for you to see. They were face to face and I think the heat here may have gummed them. I do love to see pictures of snow too. As you know I've never seen snow.

The weather here is a bit cool at nights but very hot during the day, still around 100 [38°C] most days. Autumn started last week sometime, although it still feels like summer. It is 8:30 and we have just finished morning tea. Len has taken Terry for a ride with him to Dad and Mum's place so I am writing while I have peace.

I went with Tom when he was having a practice run on the beach in his Gnat on Sunday. Enclosed is a photo I took. I clocked him as he drove (me in the Austin car) and he left me behind with my speedo showing 78 miles per hour [126 kph].

I didn't like to go any faster as the sand was rather loose. The pineapples have eased off a bit now and I have more spare time. I've been doing some gardening. Well, Fran, I guess I had better wash the dishes and prepare lunch.

So love,
Dulcie

12th April 1960

Dear Fran,

Today is very wintery here and tonight will probably be very cold. We have had a number of cold nights and I have made Terry three pairs of winter pyjamas, two pairs for Len and two for myself. Also have made two coats for Terry and have one to finish yet for myself.

We are going to a wedding on Easter Saturday and I have made a new frock - navy with a white allover lace design - have white hat and bag and navy shoes to go with it. Have made Terry blue pants and shirt with red embroidered puppies on the pockets and a red velveteen coat with gilt buttons and buckle for the belt. He also has red and blue sandals and he looks very nice in the outfit.

Yes, Fran, the southern states, Victoria, New South Wales and South Australia, have snow but not in Queensland or most of West Australia.

Len's sister Margaret and I went to Green Lake last Saturday and we caught five fish and shot ten ducks. The dog got tired of swimming for them, so I had to swim for them myself as Margaret can't swim. I really enjoyed myself. I love swimming so we plan to go again next week. Terry enjoys himself too, but mainly he likes the jeep ride. It's about 20 miles [32 km] there and back through the bush as there is no road.

Len has been going to Saltwater to fish and has caught quite a few the last few weeks. Mainly gets crabs but I like them too.

My hens aren't laying too well with the cold weather and the poor cats hate to go outside. The temp is 73 degrees [23°C] now and I am shivering.

So I had better close now and try to get some warmth into the house.

So love to all,
Dulcie

13th June 1960

Dear Fran,

Well, we are having a cold windy day today. We haven't had many frosts yet but how I hate the cold westerly winds.

Today is a Public Holiday all over Australia for the Queen's birthday. The Yeppoon show started on the 11th and we went yesterday. We had a good time. Terry enjoyed himself, ate toffee apples and fairy floss until he was so full he couldn't look at any more. Today is the last day of the show but it is so cold we won't be going again.

A Trans-Australian airliner crashed into the sea 200 miles [322 km] north of here on Saturday and killed 29 people. Among them were children and a school teacher going home for the holidays.

Also the American consulate in Queensland, Mr. O'Grady. So far 8 bodies have been recovered. Mr. O'Grady's body is to be taken back to America for burial. It was the worst crash in Australian history and the first for 14 years.

I have a pet kangaroo now. It is only a baby and I have to feed her by a medicine dropper. When she gets a bit bigger she will probably take to a bottle and teat. Dad shot the mother eating the corn near his house and kept the joey for me. She weighs only 2 and ½ pounds [1 kg] so you can imagine how big she is.

Len at the Yeppoon show

Yes, Fran, I will send you some magazines as soon as I go to Yeppoon again.

Len's birthday was on 29th May. I bought him an SLC Record player. He likes classical music and waltzes. So he can collect as many as he likes now. The radio mostly plays the Top Forty and Rock n Roll music. I like it myself - can't stand the classical type.

We are picking the winter fruit again, pineapples, pawpaws, bananas and oranges and lemons and mandarins. The peach trees are all in flower too and they look very pretty.

The State Children's Department wants us to take a little girl into our care. She is nearly two years old and an orphan. The State orphanages are too full and they want people with only a small family to take one or two of the kiddies. We haven't thought about it much yet - but I would love to take her. Of course, it depends on Len. I think she'd be a good little mate for Terry too.

Most of my friends who had babies when Terry was born are expecting again. My neighbour is expecting her 9th child.

Well, Fran, I will have to close now and get the fowl on for dinner.

So love from,

Dulcie

PS Do you collect any matchbox covers or things like cards from cereal packets and cigarettes? I have a lot of spares that I'll send you if you would like to have them. They are like the one enclosed and they have pictures of Australian birds, animals and flowers on them.

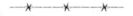

8th August 1960

Dear Fran,

Sorry I've been so long answering your letter but I've been in hospital for 5 weeks. I had an operation and got over it and eight days later got peritonitis.

It was terrible. I've never had such pain in all my life and my whole body was so swollen I looked horrific.

The doctors told Len and my family that I wouldn't live for more than two days. Len stayed with me for most of the two days, but I started to pick up a bit and the doctors said it was just luck as they couldn't do anything more.

I feel a lot better but I'm not able to get out of bed. I have 5 more weeks to stay here yet and then the doctors say I may be able to go home.

I miss Terry and Len very much. They don't get in to see me very often. It's too far and the road's too bad.

It's very cold here too. The hospital is very old and the wind blows in through the cracks in the timber. It seems to be colder during the day than it is at night.

I've started to knit Terry another jumper while I'm in here.

By the way Fran, thank you for the magazines. They arrived a couple of weeks ago and Len sent them in last week. They were nice to read while I'm lying here. When I get home I will send you a bundle.

Also Fran, many happy returns for your birthday. I'm sorry I'm not able to get out and get you a pretty card.

Mum and Dad are looking after Terry during the days and Len takes him home at night and takes him back to Mum's after breakfast. He doesn't know me and won't let me touch him when they are able to bring him in.

There is a small girl in the same room here and she is very nice and good company. They put her in here a week ago after I got okay.

She had her appendix out. But she is going home tomorrow so I'll be lonely again, unless they put someone else in.

Well, Fran, I think I'll close now and have a bit of a rest.

So love,

Dulcie

26th September 1960

Dear Fran,

Well, I'm home at last and feeling a lot better. I had to go to Rockhampton for X-rays a couple of days ago and don't know the results yet.

You really must have enjoyed your holiday at the lake. Well, just as you are coming into winter - we are on the first days of summer and very hot it has been, too. However, it looks rainy today and everybody's praying it will rain inches. Most of the livestock are dead and others just skeletons from the long drought we've had.

Yes, I'm doing some shopping for materials, too, to make up summer frocks and shorts for myself. I hope your cousin's little girl recovered from her bad burns. Burns are terrible things.

Karen would have been 4 years old on 29th September if she was alive. Mum's birthday is on the same day. I bought her a new handbag.

We had to buy a new radio last week. The old one broke down. This one is a Sanyo All Wave and we listen to Radio New Zealand, Denmark and America at nights.

We had terrific fires here last week, too. Some people had their pineapples burned out and one farm had the house burnt down too.

We didn't have anything burnt but all our water was used to help the Bush Fire Brigade.

The smoke is still very thick and we all have sore eyes from it. Our old tomcat hasn't been home since the fire so he may have been burnt. There are burnt bodies of wallabies and kangaroos, cats, birds, little animals all through the bush.

I have enclosed some match case tops of Australian fauna for you, Fran. We are members of the World Match Box Collectors Society and collect them from all over the world. If you get any tops you don't want would you let me have them please, Fran? The Australian fauna set runs up to No. 64 and I will put a few in each letter all in order.

Well, Fran, I must away now and do some work.

So love,

Dulcie

23rd October 1960

Dear Fran,

Many thanks for the match box covers. It doesn't matter what is on them, Fran, I'll be pleased to get any you send. Both Len and I smoke so we use lots of matches.

Mark must be quite a nice big boy now. Terry can talk quite well and repeats words like a parrot. He is just 3 feet [91 cm] tall and weighs 32 pounds [14.5 kg]. He takes after Len. He is 6 feet 1 inch [185 cm] tall and weighs 196 pounds [90 kg].

Enclosed is a snap of Terry taken when he was 20 months old.

The other photo is one I took from our front verandah when the bush fires were burning.

This fire was burning on the road in front of our house. The road is between the trees.

We had a thunderstorm last night but only had a light shower of rain from it. We are out of water and most of the other folks about are also out of water. We all have to go to a creek 5 miles [8 km] away and fill a small tank on the back of the truck and bring it home and pour the water into our house tanks. I don't know what we'll do when the creek dries up. It will not last too long as everyone is carting water from it. I hope it rains before the creek goes dry.

We bought Terry a pedigree Scotch collie pup last week. She is only 6 weeks old. Terry loves her and she will be good company for him when she grows up. Her name is Lady Maree of Collville, but we shortened it to Lady.

24 October (continued)

Well, I left your letter till today to finish it. We are in the midst of another storm - thunder and lightening everywhere but no rain so far. Gosh, what a noise it's making. The cat and puppy are both scared and are under the kitchen stove. Terry is half scared and half curious. There's a terrific wind blowing and I can see peaches and pawpaws blowing off the trees. The barometer reading is 29 so looks like we are in for a bad gale. I have the radio on short-wave trying to pick up the storm warning - but I can hardly hear it.

Well, I guess I'd better close and lock down the windows and doors as Len isn't home.

Love,

Dulcie

PS It's starting to rain.

6th December 1960

Dear Fran,

It is extremely hot here today and the march flies are bad. Terry is having a nap and I had to put his net down as they bite so hard.

[The females of most species of march fly take a blood meal after inflicting a painful bite with their piercing mouthparts.]

We have the Federal election coming up this Saturday. We have to vote for the next Prime Minister. I somehow don't think the present one, Mr. Menzies, will be voted in for the next term. He is a Liberal member and I think either a Country Party or Labour member will be our new Prime Minister.

Christmas isn't far off now. Terry has asked for a Road Grader instead of a pedal car now. He'll get his wish and perhaps get the car for his birthday.

We went with Len for the day last Sunday. He had to go to Rockhampton to play with the Yeppoon Cricket Team.

Terry and I watched the cricket for a while then went to visit the zoo. It was a very nice day out. We have a new short road to Rockhampton now. They have just finished putting bitumen on it.

It's only 42 miles [67 km] from here to Rockhampton now. Just 1 and ½ hours drive. The speed limit only allows one to travel at 30 miles per hour [48 kph]. The last 12 miles [19 km] is unsealed and terribly rough so it takes a bit longer to get over it. However, much better than it was before.

I'll send some papers during the next week, Fran, if I can. Our post offices here close for overseas mail on the 9th of this month. That is, of course, until after Christmas.

I had an enormous wash to do today but it's so hot the clothes were dry half an hour later.

Well, I guess I must away now and do the ironing.

Merry Christmas to you all.

Yours truly,

Dulcie

23rd December 1960

Dear Fran,

Many thanks for the parcel. I don't know what I was most pleased with, the tray or matchbox tops or papers. The tray is very beautiful and interesting. All my friends have been to admire it and are very envious. I couldn't get anything depicting Australian scenes except a handkerchief for you. However, I'll keep looking around for something.

Have a heap of match tops to send you. You seem to use book matches over there. We only have ours in small boxes with scratchers on the sides. At present they all have pictures of Australian animals and birds but in the new year they are to have Australian wild flowers on them.

Len went to Rockhampton this morning. Terry and I didn't go as we have to cart water for the sheep and cattle each day. Have two sheep on the back lawn trying to keep them alive as they are good ones and we can't let them die.

I am going to drive out to Dad's place after we get the work done as I have to help him butcher a pig for Christmas.

I iced my Christmas cake yesterday and it looks lovely. Have made the pudding and most of the patties and cakes. Haven't much to do now, only the fowl, etc.

We heard on the radio a couple of days ago that there was a bad air-crash in New York. Pictures of it were in the papers. It must have been horrible.

Am listening to the hit parade at present. Elvis Presley's "It's Now or Never" and "Are you Lonesome Tonight" are the two most popular records here now. Also "Save the Last Dance for Me" and "Please Help me I'm Falling" are quite popular.

Terry, Len and Dulcie 1960

Well, Fran I must away and get this work started on. Best wishes to all and happy returns to Mark at the end of December and also to Ricky in January.

Love,
Dulcie

17th January 1961

Dear Fran,

Well, I don't remember who wrote last but as I haven't heard from you I guess it must be my turn. Well, we had a good, though very hot start to our new year.

We had 8 inches [20 cm] of rain last week and it was very welcome.

The garden looks lovely. All the roses are in bud and there are quite a few different plants in open flower.

The pines are ripe and we have started to pick - only a few crates so far but will be going full time in a week or two.

Len with young Terry sitting on pineapples

I had to mow the lawn yesterday and it looks nice too. I have mailed you some matchbox tops and magazines. Also a big picture of Australian wild flowers.

You can either frame or hang it or roll it up and put it away. I hope it doesn't get ruined on the way over.

Terry will be two on the 20th January. We bought him a little toy barrow to help me in the garden. He always tries to push mine when it's full of weeds and soil. Now he can push his own.

I drove in to Yeppoon to have a couple of hours on the beach yesterday. Terry loved it but it was very hot and we couldn't stay long - else he would have been badly sunburned.

I have a hen sitting on 12 eggs. They should hatch on Terry's birthday. I hope to get a few chicks.

Well, Fran, must away and try to get Terry to have a sleep.

So love,

Dulcie

23rd February 1961

Dear Fran,

Gosh is it hot here! The last four days have been terrifically hot. Over 100 degrees [38°C] each day. Two weeks ago we had a terrific downpour of rain. Eighteen inches [45 cm] of rain overnight! The whole countryside was just a sheet of water when we got up in the morning. We were cut off from all others for four days - by two flooded creeks. One creek was ½ mile [0.8 km] wide and the other 10 feet [3 metres] over the bridge.

The road is just a big washout. Had to go into Yeppoon by tractor. We didn't have any damage done by the water but some people lost stock and their crops were washed away. Dad lost his old pet sheep but it came back 2 days ago. Must have been washed a long way. The water was only 18 inches from our floor (in the house) and we had 2 dogs, 1 cat, fowls and 2 sheep on the verandah.

Houses here aren't built like yours. Ours are made on high blocks 7 feet [2 metres] or 3 feet [91 cm] high from the ground depending on how low the land is. Ours is about 3 feet. Of course no one in Australia has basements as you say you have over there. I believe they have them in England too.

I must take a photo of our house to send you. I bought a colour film to take some coloured photos to send you. I haven't taken any yet. Terry has a heavy cold. He was very bad with croup last night and neither he nor I had much sleep. I made two new dresses for myself. One is a satin-striped poplin and the other embroidered nylon. The nylon is very pretty.

Australia Day was celebrated a few days ago. Australia was

discovered 173 years ago. Not very old is it? Our Governor General, Lord Dunrossil, died too a couple of days ago.

I have been doing some reading lately, "Where Eagles Gather" by Douglas Baber was one good book I read.

Our top tunes seem to be all of German origin now. Elvis Presley's "Wooden Heart" and "Sailor" by Lolita, and two others I forget what the names are. I rather like them too.

I bought an LP record of Johnny Horton last time I went to Rockhampton and I'd like to get Elvis Presley's "GI Blues".

We had to pick and crate pineapples yesterday. Gosh! It was hot work and I got a bit sunburnt. They ripen quick when the weather gets hot. Have sent 248 crates off so far - still more to go too.

Will tie up a bundle of papers to send you on Monday 27th.

I think I'll be going into town that day.

Well, Fran, I hear Len coming home for dinner so I guess I'd better close and get it ready.

Love,
Dulcie

27th March 1961

Dear Fran,

Well, it is raining again today. Gosh, it always rains when I hang the washing out.

I went to Yeppoon this morning to collect a kitten for Terry. It is pure white with lovely blue eyes. I wish he would stay small - he looks so beautiful!

Yes, Fran, I read Errol Flynn's story, "My Wicked, Wicked Ways". I thought it a disgusting lot of rot!

I read a good Australian book last week, "A Straight Furrow" by Frank Kellaway. It was very interesting.

We haven't been out much lately so we went to the pictures on Saturday night. We saw "Tammy". I liked it very much. So far "The Sundowners" hasn't been showing in Queensland.

I don't know about the southern states though.

No, Fran we don't find the American dialect hard to understand as most of the recordings come from America and also nearly all of the radio serials are American ones.

Even the children's ones, Wyatt Earp, The Lone Ranger etc. They are all made in America so we get quite used to it.

Well, I must away now, Fran, and feed the animals.

Love,

Dulcie

Tuesday 23rd May 1961

Dear Fran,

Please forgive me for not writing before this to thank you for the lovely birthday card and good wishes. Gosh, I've been sick. Could hardly get about for 3 weeks. However, I am okay now.

We are getting some cold nights here now. Winter is well on the way. We had a light frost but it didn't do any damage to the crops.

Len has been busy burning timber that he bulldozed off. We will probably plant fruit trees and pineapples in the new clearing.

Did I tell you in my last letter that we bought a new car? It is a Holden, an Australian made car - lovely too!

We are going for a trip to Mackay soon, in the Holden. We haven't had a holiday for about 4 years so we will really enjoy this one.

I have enclosed some match tops. They have pictures of Australian Wildflowers on them. If you collect them I will send you some in each letter. They are a series and go from 1 to 64 so I will try and get you a full set.

Also enclosed is a picture of part of Yeppoon beach. I took some colour pictures of Terry and Len on the bulldozer - when they come out I will send you a couple - if they are good!

Well, Fran, I must away now and finish my washing.

So all the best and love,

Dulcie

10th June 1961

Dear Fran,

Well, I hope you have received my other letter by now. I hope Dick is much better and that the cardiogram didn't show anything serious.

We are having cool weather here. Officially winter starts on 12 June. The temp was 67 degrees [19°C] this morning. Gosh! I was frozen stiff until mid-morning.

That is certainly good news about your story. I didn't know you wrote short stories. What kind Fran? Romance, adventure, murder? Gosh $75 seems a lot of money. A dollar is 10 shillings Australian.

There are 20 shillings in a pound and wages here are £12 per week. The cheapest car out here costs about £1000 and a small house about the same. Meat is 3 shillings a pound (30 cents), and bread 1 and ½ shillings a loaf (12 cents). Milk is 1 shilling a pint (20 cents a quart). So you see our money doesn't go far. A good frock costs about £10 ($20) so you can see why I make all our clothes. Dress material can be bought for 4 to 6 shillings a yard [91 cm].

Things are very bad out here too. There are thousands of unemployed. It must be very hard when one is paying a house and furniture off and loses his job as so many of the workers here are doing. We are very fortunate to have our farm. We are not in debt and don't have anything to pay off. So if we were really desperate we could live off our own produce and only have to buy a few clothes now and again.

Most of the farmers are in the same position as us. We are unable to get a market for our produce now. With so many unemployed they just haven't the money to buy much. The older folks think we are heading for another depression like they had in the early 1930's. I can see us living on fruit and beef, pork and poultry for a long time if that happens.

You say you thought the kangaroos would be bigger when

Terry & Collie 1961

you saw them at the zoo. How big were they, Fran? Out here they grow to about 7 ft [213 cm] high in a couple of years. Most stay that tall but a few old bucks grow around 8 ft [244 cm] but I've never seen any taller.

We shot a possum in the garden last night. They are eating pawpaws from a tree near the bedroom. I skinned it this morning and roasted it on an outside fire for the dog. The fire was lovely and warm and the dog enjoyed its breakfast!

Yes, Fran, I would like to go out to celebrate our 7th wedding anniversary on 10th July but I think we will be staying home. Buying the Holden took all our spare money.

Well, enough of our troubles, I suppose we could be worse off.

I have enclosed a few more cards of Australian fauna and flowers. I have the complete set - so will send a few each time I write. Hoping you are all well, I must away now.

So love,

Dulcie

PS I have sent a parcel of cards by ordinary mail.

—✶———✶———✶—

20th July 1961

Dear Fran,

Many thanks for the photos. I like your house. All the houses over here have fences around them. Don't you have fences over there?

Gosh, it's been cold here. Most of Queensland has had the lowest temp reading on record. It was down to 28 degrees [-2°C] here a week ago. I never felt so cold in my life before!

I heard on the news this morning that America is going to put a man up in a rocket again. I hope it is a successful trip for the fellow inside.

I have a boil on my second toe and gosh is it painful! It doesn't look much but it can really hurt, especially at night!

My garden is just a frosted black mess now. Gee, I could cry every time I look at it. Even the pineapples were frosted. They are black too.

I have enclosed a snap I took of Len bulldozing behind the house. I couldn't get close enough to him as he was pushing a tree over at the time.

So love,
Dulcie

. . .

PS Terry has another pet - a kangaroo rat. Len ran it down and caught it. They are like a kangaroo but only grow to one foot [30 cm] high.

12th September 1961

Dear Fran,

Well, we could do with some of the rain you were getting when you last wrote. Gosh, we are having terrific winds - has been blowing in great gusts for three days now. My garden is getting a bad time of it. Limbs are breaking off the shrubs and just about all the plants are stripped of leaves.

I had four back teeth out three days ago and gosh is my face painful. Usually they never worry me but this time I seem to have something wrong. My whole face is swollen and so sore.

You ask what Terry is interested in. Well, mostly riding his bike and pulling nuts and bolts out of old engines Len has in the shed. I guess he copies Len when he is fixing up the machinery. I'm glad you liked the cards. I have enclosed a couple more that belong to the Shell Project set. Also more of the matchbox tops.

Well, Fran, please excuse this short note but I don't feel the best and shall go and have a nap while Terry is having his.

Love and all the best,
Dulcie

25th October 1961

Dear Fran,

I was pleased to hear that Dick has a job. You will be all feeling bright for Christmas now.

Yes, we do have a Sears store here but its called Waltons-Sears. There are 18 branches of this store in Australia.

Did the kiddies enjoy Halloween? We don't have it over here.

Gosh, it is so hot and dry here. They say it's the worst drought since 1946. There are dead stock everywhere and those that are still alive are just skin and bones.

We are out of house water - all tanks empty. I am carting [water] in the truck from a well ½ mile [1 km] away and then I have to tip it into a tank here.

Len is so busy. He's trying to feed stock and water them too. Apart from the money loss, I hate to see animals die of hunger and thirst.

We have only recently gone out of pineapples and onto cattle too! We still keep a few acres of pineapples, citrus and other fruits just to fall back on.

I am enclosing a few stamps that someone may like. I haven't any new match tops. Have you any old stamps you don't want, Fran?

Both cats, the dog and Terry are stretched out on the verandah floor sound asleep. Lovely and cool out there! I think I'll join them later.

Mum bought a lovely Persian kitten. Gosh, it's beautiful but such long fur, nearly 2 inches [5 cm] long. I don't think it will be much good up here in the tropics. However, she is considering getting its fur cut.

Well, Fran, I must away now and get a cool lunch ready and then get the truck out for more water!

Yours with love,

Dulcie

2nd February 1962

Dear Fran,

Many thanks for the papers and lovely bracelet. Terry enjoys his puzzle very much. We don't see things like the bracelet and puzzle out here. I mean ones of Australia to send overseas. However I was able to find a couple of things to send with some papers a few weeks ago. You should get it soon.

You say in your letter Ricky starts school in September. Our kids start school here January 30th and go every week from 9 to 3:30. They have 2 weeks holiday in May and go again until August when they have 2 more weeks off, then go until December 18th then have a few weeks off and start again on January 30th the following year.

Children must be 5 years old before they start and they must start on January 30th and aren't allowed to start in the middle of the year. If they miss out through sickness or something they have to wait till the following year. Most country children are taught at home by their mothers by correspondence schools as there aren't many schools in the country.

Terry will be quite lucky as the school here is only 12½ miles [20 km] away and the State Government pays for a bus to take the children from this area to school. The bus passes our house and leaves here at 7:30 in the morning and gets back here at 5:30 in the evening. It's a long day for a small child though.

I think I'll wait until Terry is 6 years old. I can apply for a year's absence from school on account of the distance if I want to. At this time of the year here it's risky to send the kids when it's raining as the creeks come up and often the bus gets stranded and the kids have to be either brought over in boats or stay the night in the bus and come over the next morning if the creeks have dropped.

January, February and March are what is termed the wet season here, though monsoon rains come down from the north. The creek closest to us has been over the bridge only once this year but not high enough to stop traffic. It's very hot and steamy now - while there's a break in the rain. Len has been bogged twice today with the tractor - is he in a nice mood?!

Well, Fran, I guess I must close and do some work. So once again many thanks for the gifts and I hope you get yours okay.

Love from,
Dulcie

———✗———✗———✗———

17th March 1962

Dear Fran,

Well, we have had plenty of rain now! We have been isolated by the two creeks for a week, however they have gone down under the bridges now.

Officially summer is over and we are in autumn now. It's quite cool too, was 75 degrees [24 °C] this morning and I had to put a blanket on the beds last night.

It's a lovely day today - the sky is clear and blue and a bright westerly breeze is blowing. The temp is still only 77 [25°C] degrees at midday!

Len is away at the far end of the place ringbarking [killing trees by stripping bark around the circumference of the trunk] and he'll be there a fortnight before he comes home. Seems kind of lonely here - just Terry and I.

I have another boil on one of my toes! What a place - it's very sore and throbbed all last night.

We have to go into Yeppoon in two weeks time for our chest X-rays. It's compulsory to go every twelve months for an X-ray for TB [tuberculosis] in Queensland. I don't know about the other states - if they do or not. It's quite free, the government pays and I think it's a good idea. The only way to wipe it out. North Queensland has a very high TB rate.

Gee! I got ducklings everywhere at the moment and three other ducks are sitting. One on 20 eggs, due out in a week - one on 15 eggs and another on 13 eggs. I keep them to eat. Sometimes I sell them if I get too many.

My garden looks lovely just now. Roses and gladioli are out in bloom with countless annuals and all the bulbs to flower are starting to shoot after winter.

We've got a wonderful crop of pawpaws too! Ready to be picked and packed for market in a week or two. Also cucumbers, bananas and custard apples all ready to start on soon.

Gosh! Work again.

Well, Fran, I had better close now - by the way have you got the parcel I sent yet?

Love and all the best from,

Dulcie

PS Will have a new set of match boxes for you next letter.

23rd April 1962

Dear Fran,

Today is Easter Monday and the Easter holidays have taken a few more lives in accidents. Three car smashes in Yeppoon since Good Friday. We went into Yeppoon on Saturday and gosh was there some traffic about! The roads were full! We stayed to see the pictures and saw "Summer Place" starring Sandra Dee and Richard Egan and another one - some cowboy thing. I liked "Summer Place" very much.

Many thanks for the photos. They are a beautiful colour. Mark has an impish look about him and I bet he likes to get into mischief? Like Terry.

I have enclosed a few pawpaw seeds for you. I can't put many in the letter in case they make it too heavy. They like a tropical climate but if you put the seeds in after winter and keep them in a warm sunny spot they will come up, then the trees must be kept in a warm place too. Maybe you could plant the seed in large 4 gallon tins or something and take the trees inside in winter.

You must have a male and a female tree to get fruit to set. One male to every 10 female trees. The male tree gets long branches of flowers about 12 to 14 inches [30 - 35 cm] long and the female gets white flowers close up against the stem. The bees then pollinate them.

If there are no bees, rub flowers off the male on the females. The trees bear [fruit] when they are about 7 and 8 months old and 3 ft [91 cm] or so high. The fruit goes yellow and soft when ripe.

They grow kind of wild here. Every seed that hits the ground will grow but I don't know how they'd go in the cold areas. Anyway, try them.

About that "monster" that was found in Tasmania, it has never been released what it was! There was a fuss about it when it was found - some rumours about it being a whale and all sorts of things but I think it was more of a hoax as no pictures ever appeared in the papers.

[https://www.youtube.com/watch?v=a6O9j2Nb4KE]

Well, Fran, I must end now and get some work done. Len is away and Terry and I have the outside work to do.

Your pal,

Dulcie

PS Enclosed is a part of new set of match tops. Progress of Australia. There are 64 tops to the set. Will send the others as I get them.

—✕— —✕— —✕—

1st July 1962 Mt. Pelion Via Mackay, Queensland, Australia

Dear Fran,

You'll notice the change of address. We are up here for the sugar cane season.

Len is cutting 1900 tons [1 ton = 1016 kg] at the rate of 20 tons a day. Gosh, they are long days. Up at 4:30 am and not in bed again until 9:30 pm. Still there's a lot of money in it and we need it, to swing off the fruit crops at home onto beef cattle. We need about £2000 to buy the cattle to stock our place. It's about 300 miles [483 km] from home to here.

The cane farms have small huts on them for the cane-cutter and family to live in - and are they small! This one has 1 bedroom 10 x 20 feet [3 x 6 metres]. 1 kitchen 9 x 20 feet [2.7 x 6 metres]. 1 small verandah and a bathroom just big enough to fit in! The laundry tubs and an old copper boiler are outside and I have to wash outside, rain or shine. Still, I guess I'll suffer it 'till it's over at the end of the year.

You should see inside the hut. There is an old fridge about 14 years old that runs on kerosene, an old-fashioned type of kitchen dresser, a small pine table and three old chairs plus an old black stove that burns wood and smokes our eyes out. There were no beds so we brought our own and there's no cupboards or wardrobes to put clothes in, so they have to stay in our suitcases. The floors are bare wood and how I hate scrubbing them! Oh well, I guess its good exercise - I suppose I need it too.

The Holden all packed up to go up to Mackay

Did I tell you last letter I'm expecting a baby at the end of November? I have the same doctor in Mackay as I did when Karen was born 6 years ago. A woman doctor and she was very good so we went into Mackay last week and I went to her again. We are only 1 and ½ hours drive from Mackay - most of the road is bitumen surfaced and the road gang are working on the other few miles of gravel road.

A beach, "Seaforth" is only 10 miles [16 km] from here and we go down each weekend. We have rented a house there to spend the weekends. The house is lovely and fully furnished - a change from here.

Well, Fran, I must away now as I have to get dinner on for Len. All the best and love from,

Dulcie

5th August 1962

Dear Fran,

The weather here has been quite cold. We haven't had any frost but still the nights and mornings are very cold. The days warm up to 80 degrees [27°C]. So far this winter we've had only one frost and winter is over at the end of this month. Just as well as I certainly don't like the cold! Actually the weather is no different to home here, Fran. We are only 300 odd miles [483 km] from home.

We are going to drive down to have a look at the place this weekend. Just to see how the stock, etc. are doing. Probably won't want to come back when we see home again!

I've been in hospital for a couple of weeks. Have a duodenal ulcer and it plays up a bit with this hectic life and long days. I don't think the baby helps it either! Len really had a job while I was away. He had to look after Terry and cut cane too.

Terry followed him up and down the paddock and played in the dirt with his toys. When he got tired he went to sleep in the car. Len said he was very good. Poor little kid came in one night to see me with Len and got into bed with me and told me he was going to ask the doctor if he could take me home.

We can drive down to a beach every weekend and stay at a motel. It's a break from the hut anyway! No, Fran, there's only the people who own the farm living here and they think they are too good to speak to us. We didn't tell them we have a place 4 times as big as theirs and a lot better. If they want to think they are better it doesn't worry me.

At home we never act as if we're better than the people who

work for us if they are there at meal time - they eat with us and I find even the poorest people are very nice. But these people here are Italians so maybe in Italy they are like that.

Well, Fran, I must away now and get dinner and then we'll be off to the beach for the afternoon.

All the best and love from,

Dulcie

22nd August 1962

Dear Fran,

Belated birthday greetings. I knew your birthday was in August but I had an idea it was August 30th. Must be confusing it with someone else. You were lucky not really feeling any older.

The other day when I was talking to my mother I happened to mention something about my age. I thought I was 24 but mother said 25. When I thought about it for a while I realised she's right. I felt older straight away. Silly isn't it?

We went home for three days last weekend (Len cut on the previous Saturday and Sunday so we could have a long weekend the following week). Everything looked lovely and we hated coming back here.

We went to see my parents and Len's while we were down there. They all raved over Terry and said how he'd grown and we've only been away 9 weeks! Terry cried when we told him we had to come back here again.

It really wasn't a very profitable trip. We hit a bad grid at night (Len driving pretty fast!) and broke the main leaf in the back springs and the control arm assembly and shock absorber on left side front. Patched it up and came on again.

Later a kangaroo jumped out of the grass on the side of the road and crashed into the right-side door. We'd been dodging the confounded things on the road all night. Still later Len swung over to let a semi-trailer past and hit a large rock on the left side mudguard and door. So our lovely car is now somewhat battered.

Mother wrote today and said my eldest brother got caught in the corn-picker-thrasher. He hasn't any broken bones but has some bad bruises and in shock. They've been working flat out to harvest the maize before we get thunder-storm rain to ruin it. It appears the picker jammed and Tom crawled up to release it and his clothing got caught in some cogs. He always works with his shirt hanging out and it's always getting caught in something or other.

I've just finished doing the washing. Gee it's hard work by hand with only a wood-boiler to boil them in! I feel so tired now. I'm lying on the bed writing instead of ironing. I feel quite okay again now the ulcer hasn't played up since I've been out of hospital. My kidney troubles me a bit though.

When I was in hospital after losing the last baby I had to have one kidney and one ovary removed as the peritonitis had affected them and the remaining kidney has to work overtime. My feet and hands swell up so big. It's really alarming to see them some days. However the doctor keeps a close check so everything must be ok.

I've just about made all the baby clothes I'll need. I knitted some woolen bootees and one complete layette - but I don't think I'll need them as it will be extremely hot when baby arrives. Probably won't even need the cotton frocks I've made - just a singlet or nappy [diaper].

It's very dry here and bush fires are raging around. One farm had 300 tons [304814 kg] of cane burnt out last week. I hope none gets burnt here. We burnt fire breaks all around our place when we were home so it's quite safe. The cattle country can burn whenever its ready - was too green to burn when we tried it.

Well, Fran, I must away now and do this ironing.

Love,

Dulcie

PS About the magazines, better send them to our home address. I will get up a bundle for you, too.

3rd October 1962

Dear Fran,

Well, we are really into summer again. The days are terribly hot but the nights aren't too bad yet. Cane cutting isn't much fun in this heat. I get up each morning at 5 o'clock, get breakfast, then call Len and he goes to work at 6 o'clock - comes back for lunch and then doesn't get back until 7 o'clock in the evening. Long hours.

We sold our Holden car and bought a Ford Zephyr last week. Then we went for a drive down to home on Saturday and came back Sunday night. The worst part about going home is having to come back here again!

Mum's Persian cat had four kittens and she kept one for Terry. It was only 2 weeks old when we went down and Terry thought it was lovely but it was too young to bring back. However Len is going down at the end of this month to get mum to come up and mind Terry while I'm in hospital for the baby, so he'll get the kitten then.

I guess your boys are pleased with their puppy. Is it the first dog you have had for them? Our collie had eight pups a few weeks ago but Len killed them all as we couldn't possibly keep them.

Yes, Fran, our record player plays 78, 45, 33⅓ and 16 r.p.m. I can't say I really like Ray Charles singing "I can't stop loving you". I like Don Gibson's version better. The two songs I like most at the moment are "Roses are Red" and "Wolverton Mountain".

I've just finished scrubbing the floors. They are made of white pine and get dirty so easily but look nice after they've been scrubbed. But I still prefer the floor's covered as at home - much easier!

Gosh! I've been having kidney trouble. My feet and hands are swollen like great balloons and my back hurts every time I move! I have to go to the Doctor each week and she has given me tablets, etc. but doesn't seem to do much good. Still I've only got 5 more weeks to hang out so I guess I shouldn't complain. I don't know how big the baby is going to be but I've only gained 6 pounds [3 kg] on my normal weight and I'm still wearing my every day frocks!

We had a rather worrying time with Terry three weeks ago. He had to have anesthetic to get 6 teeth out. I took him into the hospital early in the morning and the doctor and dentist told me he'd be only 10 minutes and I could take him home again. But after they removed the teeth his breathing stopped and he had to have oxygen and resuscitation for 20 minutes to start him again.

Then he didn't regain consciousness for 5½ hours. Gosh! I thought he was dead. When he finally did wake up he just sat up in bed and said, "I think we'll go home now". Never even cried! The next day he ran around making as much noise as he usually does, while I washed, and it felt like I was 10 years older!

Well, Fran - I guess I'd better close as Terry wants a sandwich.

Lots of love,

Dulcie

12 November 1962

Dear Fran,

Well, on the day your last letter was dated - I had another son - a very small one 3 pounds 11 ounces [2 kg]. He had to have all his blood drained and replaced, because of the R.H. factor, and had jaundice very bad. He is still in hospital and will be there for 5 weeks. We named him Brendan Russell.

On the day he arrived (October 25th) I tried to wait for Len to come home for dinner, but the pains got to 3 minutes apart so Terry and I had to walk 2 miles to get him. He drove 65 to 75 miles an hour [105 - 121 kph] to get into Mackay and I just made it to the labour bed. I didn't have time to even change my clothes and he was born.

When the doctor got there 10 minutes later I had to have an anesthetic as the afterbirth wouldn't come away. The doctor told me later I had two fibroid growths growing in the womb and they had taken all the nourishment from the baby. Gosh, he's small! He's 16 inches [40 cm] long and his legs and arms are as thick as my fingers and his feet 1½ inches [3 cm] long. All his clothes are too big for him.

On the day I went in I was so worried about the trouble over Cuba. However everything seems a lot brighter now. Gosh! It's hot here now. Was 110 degrees [43°C] last Sunday and has been around 98 degrees [37°C] all last fortnight. I wish the cane was finished. It's so hot for Len cutting all day from daylight till dark. Looks like we'll be here until after Christmas and it doesn't seem the same away from home does it?

Well, Fran, I guess I'd better do some work. I was in hospital 15 days and have been here 4 days today and there seems to be endless things to do, washing, floor scrubbing and walls to clean, etc.

Lots of love,
Dulcie

PART II

1963 - 1968

29th January 1963

Dear Fran,

I must say I'm very sorry for not answering your letter before this. But so much has happened since I received your letter on 23rd December.

We were allowed to take Brendan from hospital when he was 6 weeks old - a week after we left Mt. Pelion for home. We reached home on 20th December and then I was very busy preparing for Christmas. The day we left Mt. Pelion it started to rain and we had rain all the way for the 350 miles [563 km]. Rained right through the holidays (Christmas, New Year, etc) and continued on for 4 weeks. The creeks rose over the bridges and we were isolated with only the 2-way radio to make contact with anyone. Altogether we had 35 inches [90 cm] of rain for the month so on 22nd January Len decided he'd had enough. The creeks dropped enough to let us out and we went to Rockhampton and bought a caravan and decided to clear out!

Terry and Brendan

We started out for Griffith in New South Wales. What a trip we had! We travelled 1521 miles [2448 km] over roads so bad we only made 250 miles [402 km] on some days. Took us 5 days for the trip. We didn't strike any rain after we crossed the Queensland and N.S.W. border.

Terry enjoyed the trip and Brendan slept peacefully. We brought the two cats and Terry's collie dog along in the caravan. It's very cold down here compared with home. Although it's summer it's 65 degrees [18 °C] most days and nights. The people here think its hot when it reaches 90! [32°C]

There's all kinds of stone fruits grown here. Plums, peaches, pears, etc. and we are staying to pick the fruit for the season, approximately 3 months. The wet season should be finished at home then and winter will be starting. It seems so queer here - different climate and country and crops. They say snow covers everything in winter. I would like to stay to see snow but 65 degrees [18°C] is too cold now - so I'd guess I'd freeze to death here in winter!

Brendan weighs 10 pounds [4.5 kg] now. He had another blood check yesterday but I don't know the results yet. He sleeps all night now and doesn't need night feeding. At present Len is away with some other men and Terry is asleep. Also Brendan, so I have the caravan all closed up and we are nice and warm.

The Zephyr didn't have any trouble pulling the caravan although some of the mountains were steep and high. Two of them were Chandler's Peak 5,710 feet [1740 metres] and Blackbutt ranges 4,170 feet [1271 metres]. It was lovely to look out over the country from the tops of them.

By the way Fran, thank you so much for the parcel. I will get one or two things of New South Wales to send you soon. Also just address any letters to me at Bungundarra and they will be sent on if we are still here.

Well, I've run out of paper so I must away now.

Kind regards to you all from,

Dulcie

The Zephyr, Terry and Len.

23rd April 1963

Dear Fran,

Thank you for the card and good wishes for my birthday.

I'm very sorry I've been so long writing to you, Fran, but we've had a most unhappy time since Christmas.

Brendan didn't do well and we had to take him 2000 miles [3219 km] to a specialist who put him into hospital on February 2nd. He had his blood changed twice more and had intravenous tubes in both legs and arms and oxygen until he died on March 27th.

He had leukemia and in the last 9 days of his life he developed meningitis. From then on, he didn't have a chance. We drove night and day and reached home two weeks ago. Now all our money is gone and we still owe £300 to the hospital. I just feel as if life isn't worth living. Terry misses Bren so much and keeps asking why we came home without him. He can't understand that death is so final.

We have to go back to Mackay in June to cut cane again. We need the money so badly now. I do hate it up there - but still we haven't any choice.

Please excuse me writing on both sides of the paper, Fran, but I haven't any more paper until I go to Yeppoon next week.

There's been such a lot of rain here while we were away, 80 inches [203 cm] since Christmas! Still it hasn't done any harm and the creeks and dams are full and the grass is lush. The cattle are doing well.

Terry's collie bitch is due to have a batch of pups any day and he is anxiously awaiting their arrival. His turtle also has 3 eggs and the Persian cat has had 6 kittens. We sure have a zoo!

Well, Fran, I must away now and I do hope you are feeling better now that your winter has gone. We are just getting our winter.

Love,
Dulcie

24th May 1963

Dear Fran,

Thank you for your letter and photo of Ricky. Terry liked Mark's drawing. It kept him amused for some time.

He's been very ill for three weeks and will probably have a blood transfusion next week. He's already had one. Gosh, he's lost weight and I find it hard to find anything to interest him.

He is very good though and doesn't cry when he gets his

needles. He is still missing Brendan badly too. We are allowed to bring his pets once in a while to have a look at. His old turtle has laid 3 eggs and Collie (his dog) has seven pups. Then last week Collie had two ticks on her and nearly died. However she looks okay now.

I don't know when I'll be able to go to Mackay but Len is leaving here on 7 June.

Yes, Fran, I agree with you, when you say this must be the hardest time of life. Really, I don't mind struggling along to make a living but it is disheartening to have one's children sick and also to lose them. If we lose Terry, I don't think I'd be interested in living.

I feel as if I could do with six months sleep at present. Still one thing I can't growl about - my figure. I've lost 28 pounds [13 kg] and now weigh 112 pounds [51 kg]. So worrying does some good!

Len has been doing a lot of ringbarking on our place - has about 500 acres [202 hectares] done so far and has 1000 acres more to do. Killing the timber off improves the grass.

The breeder cows are starting to drop their calves but the dingos are very bad so I guess we'll lose some. Len has been putting out strychnine baits and has caught a few young dingos. The mother ones are the worst killers when they have young ones to feed.

I've just finished spraying my garden. Grubs have been eating my roses badly. They are blooming beautifully, too.

We went to the pictures last Saturday night. First time for eighteen months. We saw, "Lonely are the Brave" starring Kirk Douglas. It wasn't very good though.

Well, Fran, Len will be home soon as it is 6:30 now so I must away.

I'm sending you some magazines tomorrow.

Love,

Dulcie

5th August 1963

Dear Fran,

I'm very sorry to have taken so long to answer your last letter. Thank you very much for the recording. We enjoyed listening to it.

I haven't had much spare time as we are in the north for the cane season again. Len has a smaller cut this year as the weather wasn't favourable to grow the cane at the beginning of the year. We expect to be finished early in November. I've been away for 2 weeks. I had to drive 650 miles [1046 km] to take Terry to a bigger hospital for a blood transfusion. Len couldn't get the time to go with me. I didn't have any trouble on the way except for the fuel pump on the Zephyr. The pipe broke in half on some bad road. I cut it and joined it again until I got to a town. One section of the road is very lonely, 250 miles [402 km] inland with not even a house in sight. I carried a spare tin of petrol as there isn't any petrol stations either. I took 2 spare tyres but didn't get a puncture. I was pleased about that as I hate changing tyres.

Terry is looking a bit better although still losing weight. He also has a very bad cold and cough.

When I can get the time I've been knitting. I've done two long-sleeved cardigans for myself and two long sleeved pullovers for Terry and I am halfway through one for Len.

It has been the coldest winter on record here. Down to 15 degrees [C]. The car's radiator is frozen every morning and the windscreen freezes over when Len goes to work. I've never felt so cold in my life.

My eldest brother is in hospital at home. He had an accident when felling trees with his chainsaw and the chainsaw fell and half cut through one foot. It's too far to drive down to see him but I phoned mother and she said he is doing well.

Well, Fran, I guess I'd better get dinner started so lots of love to you all from,

Dulcie

———✳———✳———✳———

13th August 1963

Dear Fran,

Well, winter has gone and we've had inches of rain. Len couldn't get the trucks onto the paddock to cart the cane, so we decided to go home for a few days. The road was in a terrific mess with semi-trailers bogged for a mile and cars and caravans bogged everywhere. The Roads Department had a bulldozer and a grader to pull them out. We got through okay and then 90 miles [145 km] from home Len crashed into a 12-inch [25 cm] bridge post. Terry was asleep in the back seat and wasn't hurt. It hit on my side and threw me into the dashboard. I've got a cut and bruised forehead and one arm and leg bruised and Len wasn't hurt. The car was in a bit of a mess. Gee, I got a fright when it hit the post. The post was set three feet [91 cm] deep in concrete and it cracked right out. Len was doing about 50 mph [80kph] at the time. We had to use the jack to jack the bodywork away from the wheels so we could go again. We came back to Mt. Ossa and now the car is in Mackay to be repaired.

I hope you have a good birthday, Fran, and now I must away and do some washing.

Love from,
Dulcie

18th September 1963

Dear Fran,

I was so pleased to get your letter. It gets rather lonely here, the owners' wives don't speak to the workers and the other workers' wives won't live in the small huts here, so I've got quite a way to go to find any women companions.

The workmen were bringing their washing for me to do and also dropping in for meals. I had so much to do I soon refused to do any washing and cooking for them. I put up with this horrible way of living to look after Len, so I think the other women could do it for their husbands too. We should be finished in two months time. Gee, I'd hate to spend Christmas here.

I went into the hospital for a week to have an operation on my ears. Gosh, they are sore. I can hardly bear to listen to Terry speaking. I wanted to leave it until we were finished and home again but the doctor said it had to be done immediately.

Len took Terry to work with him and did some of the washing while I was away. It was hard for Len though as Terry soon gets bored watching him work and he usually sleeps for 2 and ½ hours each day. Len said when he was tired he curled up in the grass with the collie dog. Poor kid!

We do such long hours - up in the morning at 4:30 and we don't finish work until 6:30. By the time I get tea and we are bathed it's quite late when we get to bed. So Terry certainly needs his sleep in the daytime.

How are you doing since Dick started his own business? I wish he could come and landscape all my garden! I did some of it at home but it's quite heavy work carting earth and stones and cement. We have about 3 acres [1.2 hectares] of lawn with flowering trees, shrubs and roses. Since we've been away it looks rather neglected but it won't take much cleaning up again.

My mother has a birthday on the 29th this month. I can't think what to buy her. I'll go to town next week and have a look in the shops. Our little girl, Karen, would have been seven years old on the same day. Brendan would have been 1 year old in a month's time - same day as my brother's birthday.

What are you getting the children for Christmas, Fran? I don't know what to get Terry - he has asked Santa to bring him a balloon! He just blows them up and sticks a pin in them to hear the big bang! He has a trike, a pedal car and a two-wheeled bike as well as numerous trucks, cars, bulldozer and things, so I just don't know what to get. He got a train set last year.

Maybe a new pet might be okay. He wants a pair of guinea pigs so I'll have to find out where to buy them.

Well, Fran, I must get some sandwiches cut for tomorrow and then go to bed.

Love from,

Dulcie

PS I think I can remember singing "Tie me Kangaroo Down" when I was a kid.

It ends with the words:

> "We tanned his hide when he died, Clyde,
> and that's it hanging on the shed."

Is that the same song?

10th October 1963

Dear Fran,

We seem to have had a sudden change back to winter. It is bitterly cold, with a fine rain and gusty winds. Has been like this for a week now. Len is still working because he wants to be finished in 6 weeks time. The sugar mills close the first week in December so we will be home for Christmas.

We have at last paid up all our medical and hospital accounts, £356 in all. Terry's last blood test showed an improvement and my ears are better. So looks as if we'll give the doctors a miss for a while!

We are buying another block of land, 1500 acres [607 hectares]. It joins our place and will be very handy.

How lovely it must be to see TV. So far there are only two TV stations in Queensland. Both in Brisbane and too far away to pick up any programmes. But there is some talk of one being built at Rockhampton so we might see it yet!

In 1965 Australia's currency is to be changed from pounds, shillings and pence to dollars. It's going to take me quite a while to get used to spending dollars and cents, etc.

Len and a few of his mates want to know if you could tell us what happened to the US Air Force pilot named Powers who was shot down over Russia some years ago and later returned to USA. Most people have the idea that he was tried and executed in the States for giving away secrets to Russia. [Francis Powers died in a helicopter crash, aged 47, in 1977.]

By the way, I've meant to ask you many times, do you pronounce your name as we do, that is omitting the 'e' in Globke? Ours is spoken just as Clark. Both my grandparents and Len's came from England to settle in Australia in the 1880s. Have your ancestors been long in America?

Well, I guess I'd better get Terry something to eat now he is awake.

Lots of Love,
Dulcie

24th January 1964

Dear Fran,

I've just received your letter - I do hope you'll forgive me for not writing before Christmas. I sent you a Christmas card and a photo booklet of Mackay before the end of November. You didn't say if you received it. I didn't get your Christmas card either.

After we left Mackay on December 2nd we came home for a few days and then went south to Griffith to have a stone erected on Brendan's grave. We stayed there 3 weeks and then towed the caravan home along the New England Highway. We took 6 days travelling all day and half the nights. We couldn't take our time to enjoy the journey as the drought has affected our property rather badly. Surface water is all gone and the grass is dry.

Our main concern is to keep fires from burning us out. We've lost a few cows and some calves. I have five motherless calves here at the house and I'm milking 3 cows that have lost their calves and feed the five little ones with a bottle and teat. I had seven but dingos killed two a few days ago. We poisoned their remains and the following night the dingos came back and ate it. We found 4 dead dingos so that got rid of some of the cruel things.

One of my ducks hatched out 20 ducklings last week and two more ducks should be through sitting in two days. So I'll have more "babies" to look after. Collie (the dog) had 8 pups on Christmas day too.

Our car has been out of action for a week. I did the gear box in when I went for a day to town. We had it towed home and Len has almost got it fixed again. Should be going in an hour or so. We were told that Zephyr's have a weak gear box. So next time we will buy Australia's own car - Holden - it is supposed to stand up to our bad roads better than any overseas make.

I do hope Rick improves after his operation. I know how you must worry, Fran, but I'm sure he will be okay. Will Mark be going to school this year? Terry won't be going until he is 6 next year.

He had a little party on Monday. Just a few little cousins and his grandmother and grandpap. He blew all his candles out in one puff. I made his cake and iced it. Was the shape of a well with green jelly for water and a chocolate frog coming out of the water. I used plastic flowers to trim the side of the well. The kids loved it.

There are a few clouds in the sky today. How I wish it would rain. The temp stands at 105 [41°C] each day but we haven't even had a thunder storm.

Mother just arrived from town. She brought the mail. Thank you very much for the papers, ash tray and money. I've often wished I could send you some of our money, specially as it will no longer be in use next year. I have applied for a permit to send a few pennies and shillings to you but so far I haven't been given permission to do so.

Well, Fran, I must close now and I do wish you all the best.

Love,

Dulcie

9th March 1964

Dear Fran,

I do know just how you feel about the "Beatles" records. I hate the sight and sound of them. Of course I haven't seen them on TV (I never see TV at all) but the pictures of them in magazines make me mad. I could get hold of them and give them a good hair cut.

Yes, Fran, I have received your Christmas card. They both seemed to have got lost.

We have had a very worrying time over my brother Brian. My eldest brother Tom and Brian were loading logs with the end loader on their tractor. As Tom put the lift up to get the log onto the truck it slipped out of the hooks and crushed Brian onto the ground. One leg from the thigh down is badly crushed and the doctors want to amputate the foot. Brian won't let them. He said he wants it set no matter how broken it is. I don't blame him as I would hate to lose a foot. He was to get married on March 28th.

I've enclosed some stamps for Ricky and Mark (when he starts his book). I've started one for Terry but he's only got 980 stamps so far. I'd be grateful for any used ones for him, Fran. Also enclosed, a snap of Terry and his horse.

We have had a couple of inches [5 cm] of rain during the last week. The cattle will start to pick up soon now. We want to sell some at the end of April.

Well, Fran, I must away now as I've got ducks, fowls, birds, dogs, cats and calves to feed.

Lots of love,
Dulcie

24th April 1964

Dear Fran,

Many thanks for the birthday card. It was lovely to get it as no-one else thought of my birthday. Mum did the next day but Len still hasn't so I haven't bothered to remind him.

I've been rather sick lately - had a bad cold with a touch of pneumonia. I still feel like crawling into bed and staying there. Usually I take no notice of a cold but I've had this one for 3 weeks and feel sore all over and have a terrific headache. I've neglected the house and it's in an awful mess. I'm also two weeks behind with Terry's lessons. I think I told you before that he does school from the Radio School Service and Correspondence Primary School. He was enrolled late in February. I wasn't going to start him till next year but he wanted to, so now I'm flat out all day teaching him as well as doing all my other work.

Thank you for the stamps, Fran. I haven't got around to looking for any for Ricky and Mark. However I managed to get some rare Malaysian ones - only a few were issued (the purple and yellow Malaysia one is rare). Terry is coming along fine with his collection.

Had 20 ducklings hatch out last Friday but they seem to have something wrong with them as each day a couple of them dies. I've only 14 of them left now.

Tomorrow is Anzac Day in Australia. It is a public holiday to honour the dead from both world wars. School children join members of the Armed Forces to march through the streets to the Cenotaph where wreaths are placed.

Well, Fran, I seem to be making a lot of mistakes with this letter so I think I'll close and lie down for a while.

Lots of love from,

Dulcie

20th May 1964

Dear Fran,

Thank you for the cards - the album is filling up now.

I do hope you and the boys enjoy the day at the farm and of course the horse ride! Terry is not really a fan of horses as they just mean work for him. He has no choice but to ride when I go out. His horse is a lovely little pony too and most of the city children enjoy a ride on her when they visit. We had a two-day round up for tick dipping last week and Terry was heartily sick of riding by the time we had finished. He can ride really well too but tries to keep up with me or Len but our horses out-gallop his and he gets mad! When we slow down for him he comes galloping in a cloud of dust yelling his head off because we left him behind. I've got rather a sore spot since my horse took a short cut around a tree and my boot caught the full force of it. So do be careful if you get the chance to ride on the farm.

I'm awaiting the arrival of the veterinary surgeon today. Quite a few of our young heifers have came down with a spreading disease and we have to try for something to control it before we lose any more.

Please excuse Terry's scribbling on the paper, Fran. He never lets me write in peace. Yes, he is in First Grade and can print letters very good. He has to do quite long sentences and count to 50 and do sums. He likes it so that's a help. But goodness, I never seem to have any spare time.

I envy you the lovely flowers you have. My garden looks sadly neglected. Leaves have fallen all over the lawn and weeds are everywhere. I did enjoy the five-acre [2 hectares] lawn and garden I built years ago. But now it is neglected it looks terribly untidy. I wish I could employ someone to do the housework, cooking, washing, etc. and all the cattle work, and teach Terry, and then I'd have all day for the garden. What a lovely thought!

It's been raining for two days and it is still coming down. We should be right for winter feed now. We hope to sell bullocks after winter if they are in good condition.

Well, Fran, I must away now and clean up the house before the vet gets here.

So all the best to you and the family.

Love,

Dulcie

———✳———✳———✳———

8th July 1964

Dear Fran,

Sorry I've taken so long to answer your last letter. Thank you very much for the Kennedy Stamp. I had read that it was to be issued but didn't like to ask you for one. The snaps of the boys are very good. I think Ricky must be like Terry - always puts on a silly face when I want to photograph him and in most snaps he looks like a clown.

Both Len and I have been laid up for the last month. We bought some very wild zebu cattle and had to muster them to dip for ticks. I've never seen anything so wild. We couldn't handle them and when they broke away at the yards, my horse fell while galloping and left me on the ground after she got up. I had a very sore back and a few internal injuries. Len's horse fell soon after and he has 2 broken ribs. We will have another go at them in a few weeks time.

If we manage to yard them, we are going to put them straight into the semi-trailer and take them to the sale yards. They are the first and last zebus we'll buy. The Hereford and shorthorn are so quiet we can yard them on foot.

Winter is nearly half over and we've had 3 frosty mornings. We thought it would be a rather severe winter as it was so dry. However last week rain came and we've had 6 inches [15 cm] and its still lightly showering. So feed and water are plentiful once again.

We bought Terry a pair of guinea pigs last week. What with dogs, cats, birds, goldfish and a dozen other pets he has quite a zoo now. At least the goldfish and guinea pigs don't cost much to feed. His turtle laid 4 eggs under the tank but we haven't a father turtle so I guess they won't hatch.

I'm busy knitting in my spare time. Done one long-sleeved polo-necked jumper [sweater] for Len and a cardigan for myself and have almost finished a cable-stitched pullover for my brother. He is to be married on August 15th. I do hope nothing happens to postpone it again. Just remembered Len and I have been married 10 years today. We both forgot it. Gee, makes me feel old. Guess I look as old as I feel anyway. After all in three years time I'll be 30.

Oh well, I'd better get dinner started so all the best, Fran.

Love from,

Dulcie

5th August 1964

Dear Fran,

I hope you are getting cooler weather by now. I do wish some of your nice hot days would come over here. We've had two weeks of frosty nights now and I've hardly slept. Our houses are built to be cool for summer and when we get frost we almost freeze. Two of Terry's goldfish died with the cold and I've kept hot water bottles around the tank with the others in.

Len has been gone a week today. I miss him so much. I guess that sounds silly after ten years of marriage but I'm so lonely I just don't feel like doing any work, although there's heaps to do. Terry and I mustered the cattle yesterday and dipped them and branded a few new calves, but today I haven't moved out of the house.

Your new car must be lovely Fran. We never see cars like it out here. They are mainly Holdens and British makes. There are a few American ones, Ford, Dodge and Chrysler but nothing very big and expensive.

I did ask a few children from joining properties if they would like to write to your niece, Fran, but most kids seem to have too much to do or are too shy to write or otherwise just plain lazy.

One of my ducks started to sit on eggs yesterday. I didn't want any more ducks so I put 16 hen eggs under her and took her own eggs away. She will be in for quite a surprise when her "babies" hatch.

Well, I think I'll close Fran, I can't think of anything to write about and I've got a blinding headache - had it for two days. I guess I've been smoking too much this last week.

Lots of Love,
Dulcie

23rd September 1964

Dear Fran,

Thank you very much for your letter and the lovely card. I've been feeling dreadful as I completely forgot to post your birthday card. I think I told you before that a mail transport delivers and collects our mail once each week as we live too far from a post office to post and collect ourselves. I forgot to hand the card to the driver two weeks running and then I hadn't heard from you for quite a while and I thought you must have been offended and it would be insulting to mail it so late. Please forgive me, Fran, and I do hope you had a happy day and I really did think of you. I'm mailing you a Christmas parcel next week and I won't forget this time!

It's good to know Dick's business is turning out well. You ask how the cattle business is going. Well, I guess it's okay. There's plenty of money in it but hard work and with Len not here I'm almost worn out looking after everything. The ticks are bad now with summer coming on and a blight in the eyes is also a problem. I've been branding and giving the young calves blackleg injections this past week. I've almost got that finished, only about 100 more to do. I haven't dehorned any - that will have to wait until summer is over as flies are too much of a problem now.

The cave you visited in Kentucky must have been lovely. I would love to see it. I have a hope we may be able to in 3 or 4 years time. One of our friends is going to the USA in November and wants us to go with her for the 2 months. However just now we need the money and I think Terry would enjoy it better when he's older. Do you think you'll ever make it out to Australia? I would love to meet you.

Terry's budgies hatched out - three new ones - and he's very proud of them. Also the goldfish laid eggs and seven young fish came out.

I do hope Mark likes going to school. Terry loves doing his. Of course he doesn't have to leave home but he will next year. I'm not able to find the time to teach him properly so we will have to put him in a boarding school next year. I hate to think of him going as I will miss him dreadfully.

Well, Fran, I must close now and do some ironing before I go to bed as it is 10:30 now.

Lots of Love from,
Dulcie

1st November 1964

Dear Fran,

Well, Christmas is only eight weeks away and I'll soon have to start shopping and baking the cakes. Terry wants Santa Claus to bring a 20-inch [50 cm] bike and various other things. What do Ricky and Mark want? Terry will also get a "bonus" gift. My little saddle mare is expecting a foal about Christmas time. I had her mated to an Arab stallion and I told Terry he could have the foal.

Len should be home in about 5 weeks. I hope to have all the dipping, branding, etc. done by then.

You asked if we had help, Fran. Well, no, we don't employ anyone. Len has to cut cane to get ahead a bit and we just don't have the extra money to pay anyone to help while he is away. I can handle most of it myself - sometimes I get so tired though. Out of bed at 5 o'clock every morning and not finished the work until 10 o'clock at night. I don't mind branding the calves but I hate castrating the young bull calves.

Terry's school work had to be dropped but I'm not worried about it as he will be going to school in Yeppoon next February. The State government has agreed to pay half the cost of running a bus to and from school each day to collect the 14 children between here and Yeppoon. The three other families and us are to pay the other half - which is not bad.

I smashed our Zephyr car up last Sunday night. Hit a kangaroo when Terry and I were coming home from the far paddock. Smashed in all the bonnet [hood], mudguard [fender], grille and headlights. Killed the 'roo anyway so that's one less grass-eater. I wish the scientists would hurry up and invent some disease to spread among the 'roos to kill them out. They are terrible pests - eat more grass than the cattle. Terry's pet one keeps the lawn mowed perfectly - so I guess that's all they are good for.

Well, Fran, I must close and go to bed as its nearly midnight and I have a full day tomorrow. I hope you get the parcel of Christmas presents I sent you in time for Christmas.

Lots of love from,
Dulcie

13th January 1965

Dear Fran,

Well, Christmas is over once again and we had a very busy time. Didn't feel like Christmas really. Len came home Christmas Eve night and we spent the day at home watching Terry play with his presents. Boxing day we spent riding about repairing boundary fences and have been looking for missing stock ever since.

We've had a terrific summer. Has been around 102 to 107 [39°C to 42°C] most days and the week before Christmas a bushfire burnt us out and most of the fences were badly damaged. We found some bodies of cattle that had been caught by the fire. Most of the cattle are weak from want of water and feed and if rain doesn't fall within a week we will lose heavily.

Today has been about the worst day we've ever had. Len was riding a new gelding he'd just broken in and it played up all day. Bucked, kicked and bit every time he got off it or tried to get back on it. He ended up walking and leading the horse most of the day, so we didn't get much work done.

I received the magazines you sent, Fran, they had come unwrapped and were rolled up and tied with string. The three little cards "Birds of North America" were placed in an envelope and posted from the Postmaster at the Brisbane Post office. I do hope the parcel I sent you arrived in better condition. One of Terry's guinea pigs had 4 babies last night. They are lovely little things.

Things look pretty bad here at the moment. War with Indonesia [Vietnam] is expected within the next few weeks and all boys of 20 to 25 years are being called up for the Army. I guess it will be a race to see who can bomb who first.

Well Fran, Len and Terry have long since gone to bed so guess I'd better follow. Write soon and tell me about your Christmas celebrations.

Love,
Dulcie

27th January 1965

Dear Fran,

Well, Terry started school last week. I took him in the first day and he came home on the bus in the evening and is going in and out and enjoys the bus ride. Some of the children were crying when we were waiting to enrol but Terry loved it right from the start.

He is starting to droop a bit now though - the heat combined with the bus ride of 48 miles [77 km] a day and the long day on top of it. He leaves home at 7:30 and the bus returns here at 5 in the afternoon. I feel so lonely now without him - even his dog misses him! Guess I'll have to have another baby to keep me company.

My little mare had her foal 3 days ago. It's a lovely little thing and very quiet. The mother lets me touch it but doesn't let Len or anyone else to go near. I promised it to Terry before it was born so now he will have to make friends with it and get it to follow him about. Of course it can't be broken in until it's 2 years old.

Terry's guinea pigs also had babies. Three mother ones had 10 babies between them. They are really lovely little mites.

Terry was thrilled with the idea that your boys had play-motors for their bikes. I tried all the shops in Rockhampton for one for him but alas, no one has heard of such things out here. Terry can ride the bike no trouble now - had a few falls at the start - but soon mastered it. It is a 24-inch [60 cm].

He had his 6th birthday a week ago and received lots of toys and things from his grandparents and others. I made him a big Teddy Bear cake, 18 inches long and 11 inches wide [45 cm by 28 cm]. Gee, it looked lovely. I hope Ricky enjoyed his birthday.

We still haven't had any rain since the fire and we are in a desperate position for water and grass. Len has the boring machine going, night and day, frantically trying to hit water, but water seems to be a long way down here. He bored down 120 feet [36.6 metres] and hit solid rock and had to pull out and try another place. Since the end of November the temp hasn't been below 98 degrees [37°C] during the day and most days it's around 105 [41°C].

We have been felling trees for the cattle to eat the leaves and my hands are massed with blisters from holding the chainsaw all day. I've often felt like giving up but when I see the cattle - just bones with skin on - I realise I'm not as bad as they are and get a new burst of energy.

I wonder sometimes if there's any sense battling on like this. It would be easier to give up the lot and live in town but we just keep on for Terry's sake, hoping to build up a place for him when he's older.

Half the plants in the garden are dead and the lawn is so dry a dropped cigarette butt will set it on fire.

Well, Fran, I do hope your new year started off better than it has here and do write soon as it is the only happy thing to look forward to at the moment.

Lots of love,
Dulcie

19th February 1965

Dear Fran,

It is now midday and I've just come in from working, have made coffee and a sandwich. Gee, it's lovely to sit down for a few minutes. I had a terrific headache from the noise of the chainsaw I think. Still felling trees for fodder. We've given up hope of ever seeing rain again. Today there is a terrific hot north wind blowing and with the temp 102 [39°C] everything seems to be burning up a bit more.

My brother's wife, Ann, is expecting a baby in July and at night I'm making clothes for the infant. Ann can't sew or knit and won't try. I've only one little jacket to finish knitting and that will be the last I'm doing for her. Have done 8 pairs of booties, 3 coats, 3 bonnets and sewed 3 dresses and 4 nighties. Ann isn't very pleased about the coming baby. She didn't want children for 3 years yet. I think she is very childish to carry on like that but I can't say anything to her. Perhaps she will change when the baby arrives.

Terry was very excited when I told him you had sent him a motor like your boys have. Thank you very sincerely, Fran. Yesterday afternoon Terry rode his horse down to Len after school and the horse fell in a hole. Terry hit the ground rather hard and has a fair bit of skin missing. However he wouldn't stay home from school today so he mustn't be feeling too bad.

In your letter, Fran, you asked about the ready-mixed foods. Well, I did try a few of the cake mixes but didn't care for them as they all tasted the same and I've never tried any other kind of food mix. I really don't mind cooking.

Len bought me a new stove a few weeks ago. It is an Aga slow combustion and burns coke. It has a big oven, specially for bread, and another all-purpose oven. It has its own hot water system so there's hot water aplenty with no extra cost. Two small scoops of coke keep it hot for 24 hours. Coke is £8 per ton [1016 kg] and a ton lasts 1 year without letting the stove go out. It's very cheap to get hot water and continuous heat all year for £8. The cost of the stove is rather a lot though - £540. Still it's wonderful to come home and find the stove and oven hot and water ready for baths.

The stove is beautifully finished in black and white enamel with chrome touches here and there and measures 4 feet 6 inches [137 cm] long and 30 inches [75 cm] deep. We had a terrific time unloading it off the truck and getting it inside. It weighs 12 hundredweight [610 kg]. I see some storm clouds gathering in the southwest. How I hope we get it! I wouldn't mind if it rained 20 inches [45 cm] and flooded us out.

We went to town last Monday for our TB [tuberculosis] X-rays and I got a few things to make up a parcel to send to you. About the X-ray, Fran, do you have it over there? Every 2 years everyone over 14 years of age is compelled to have a chest X-ray to see if they have TB. If the X-ray shows it's positive, the person is put into a sanitarium to be cured. Years ago the disease was very common but now, due to the X-rays and treatment, it's very rare. Also vaccination against polio and diphtheria is compulsory. I think it does help to keep these terrible illnesses down.

Well, Fran, I guess I'd better go back and do some work.

So lots of love to you all.

Dulcie

———✗——————✗————✗———

13th April 1965

Dear Fran,

It must be weeks since I received your last letter - please forgive me for not writing sooner. Terry received the motor you sent and he is so pleased. He can't wait to get home in the evenings to play with it. He showed it to the children on the school bus yesterday and every child wanted one! I love the way the little "spark plugs" light up. I wonder why Australia is so behind in getting new types of toys. Most of the toys here are about the same as when I was a child.

I've enclosed some stamps for the boys. How are their collections coming along?

I hope you can follow this writing, Fran. I cut the end off the first finger of my right hand last week and it's awkward trying to hold a pen. I was putting a new muffler and exhaust pipes on the car and one pipe had to fit inside the other. So I held onto the join and hammered the end with a piece of wood.

The pipe went into the other one alright, with the end of my finger inside it. Cut through the nail and was hanging by the skin. I tied it up and finished getting the pipes connected to the car and drove into the doctor. He stitched it on again so I hope it grows back.

We went to the pictures last Saturday night. First time for nearly a year. Terry loved it. There were two cowboy pictures on but I can't remember the names of them. I thought they were rather silly.

The ducks are all starting to hatch out their young and we have little yellow ducklings everywhere. They are so lovely when they're small. We also are getting overrun with guinea pigs. Terry started off with 3 females and 1 male just before Christmas and now we have 21! Len was saying he wished the cattle would breed as fast.

They are not doing too bad now though we lost a lot when the fire went through. Last year Len bought some Santa Gertrudis - a breed the American King Ranch Company brought out from America. They are lovely beasts. Dark red all over and very fast growing. Only trouble is they can jump over 8-foot [2.4 metres] high fences.

Have enclosed a snap of my mare and her foal when it was just born in January. The stallion was a dapple grey Arab and the foal has now changed to that colour. The mare is black and white. She's usually more red colour from rolling in our red soil!

Terry is awaiting Easter. He loves Easter eggs! He has a holiday Good Friday, Saturday, Sunday and Easter Monday. Then another the following Monday - Anzac Day. Also May 5th Labour Day. The 7th anniversary of Karen's death. Seven years sounds a long time but it doesn't feel that long since it happened.

Well, Fran, I must close and get some ironing done. Sore finger or not it has to be done.

Lots of love from,

Dulcie

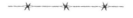

28th May 1965

Dear Fran,

Our winter has started and how I hate it! 43 [6°C] degrees this morning. However, it's back around 70 [21°C] now (midday). I've just made Len a birthday cake, he will be 37 tomorrow. Guess I'd better not put that many candles on the cake though! For my birthday last month, Len bought me a new watch. So far I haven't got anything for him though. I may take a drive into town tomorrow and get something.

By the way did I thank you for the card you sent me? I can't remember if I wrote you since my birthday. I seem to have lost track of time lately. I owe you dozens of letters. Some folks I haven't written to since Christmas.

You must have had a lovely time at the Tulip festival, Fran. How I'd love to see all those beautiful flowers! Are you going to celebrate your 10th wedding anniversary in any special way? Our 11th comes up on July 10th but guess we'll both forget like we usually do.

My brother's wife had twin boys last Sunday. One weighs 3 pounds [1.4 kg] and the other 5 and ½ pounds [2.5 kg]. They are doing well. The doctor was about as shocked as Ann when two were born. I don't think much of him for a doctor. Ann named them Kenneth Brian and William Robert.

I think your idea of a course in fiction writing is a good one, Fran. Wish I had time to take a course in diesel mechanics. Diesel engines are about the only thing that stumps me. They are just too complicated! However they are better than petrol motors and we must have them.

Well, there's no news here so I guess I'll close and go around the dingo baits. Might find a few dead ones.

Lots of love,
Dulcie

19th July 1965

Dear Fran,

You and the children must certainly be enjoying the holidays. I wish we could find time to enjoy ourselves. The years are flying away and all we seem to do is work, work, work. We celebrated our 11th wedding anniversary on July 10 putting up a new dividing fence. Very enjoyable time I must say. Len went to Mackay to cut cane again, so I won't see him till November. Ah, I feel in a miserable mood now - maybe things won't look so bad tomorrow.

We've had a few frosts, nothing really like winter though, and the days are quite warm, mostly about 80 degrees. [27°C]

I've done a bit to the garden in the last week. Most of the roses are in bloom, also gerberas and hibiscus - however everything else has lost their leaves till spring. I mowed half an acre [0.2 hectares] of lawn and will finish the rest tomorrow. Looks lovely when it's mowed, wish I could keep it neat all the time. At nights I've been knitting and made a long-sleeved polo-necked pullover for my brother, Tom.

Brian's wife brought the twins home on Friday. They are 2 months old now. One weights 7 pounds 9 ounces [3.4 kg] and the other 6 pounds 9 ounces [3 kg]. Their new house isn't quite finished yet so they are living with Mum and Dad. Mum says the babies cry nearly all night so I guess everyone will have short dreams for awhile.

Terry hasn't been too well lately. Took him to the doctor last Friday and he has to have an X-ray this Friday, Doctor thinks he may have sinus trouble - unusual for one so young.

Yes, Fran, the children do print differently. Terry is not supposed to be still printing. They do writing in the second year but he finds it easier to print. He says he will write the boys a letter this time. Will probably take him all day.

Well, I must go to bed so will finish this tomorrow.

21st July

Didn't get around to writing yesterday - was too cold. We had the coldest night on record for the central district. Snow fell only 80 miles [129 km] away. First time in history. You should see the garden, just a black mess and no flowers now! Two baby calves I had tied up near the car shed were frozen dead.

Did I say it was nothing like winter? Sleet is forecast for today. I've never seen sleet or snow so guess it will be an eye-opener if we are brave enough to go out.

The school closed for today as the children would probably freeze. None of the houses or schools, shops, etc. are heated here. Not considered necessary.

Terry and I are tucked into a bed we put up in the kitchen and have the stove coked full. Locked the dogs in the car shed along with guinea pigs, ducks, fowls, etc. I hope the poor things don't freeze to death. Guess we'll lose a few head of cattle. Heard on the radio that hundreds of sheep were frozen to death yesterday in the snow. As if a drought wasn't enough hardship now this to top it off.

Well, Fran, I'd better close as Terry is complaining that I'm letting the cold under the blankets.

Lots of love and hope to God we are still alive tomorrow,
Dulcie

PS The mail transport probably won't be along today to get this anyway.

25th October 1965

Dear Fran,

I think the last time I wrote you was sometime in August. I hope you didn't think I'd forgotten you. Time has been against us and there's been no time for writing.

We had a terribly hard winter and suffered heavy stock losses and to top it off there's been no rain since. The whole of Queensland and New South Wales are drought struck and the stock losses have amounted to hundreds of thousands. Out of 300 head of cattle we now have the grand total of 60 left. I've been working like a madman trying to fell trees for them to eat the leaves and carting 1000 gallons [3785 litres] of water a day - had to fence up all the water holes and dams - as the weak cattle were bogging.

Out of bed at 4 o'clock each morning to get part of the work done - return to the house at 7 to get Terry bathed, dressed and breakfast and onto the bus at 7:30, then back into the house and off again.

Return at 5 to meet the bus and take Terry with me again to finish off. Then home at 8 pm to get Terry bathed and fed and into bed. Then all the house animals and fowls and ducks, etc. fed and the housework and cooking done for next day. Into bed at midnight and up again at four and on it goes again.

Despite all this there's only 60 head of cattle left. The hardest part is having to shoot the ones that are down and too weak to get up. The way the poor things look at me as I stand over them with the rifle. I usually end up crying after I've shot a few. This has been going on for weeks now and I still can't harden myself to this task.

The government is at last going to offer some assistance to the cattlemen to help save some stock by setting up a drought relief fund. Why they had to wait till nearly everything's gone is hard to understand. Hatred of the Prime Minister, Mr Menzies, is high in three states and now he has had his bodyguard increased to 30 men to accompany him everywhere.

The only thing he appears to be interested in is Royalty and thinks nothing of inviting the Queen or others of the Royal family to tour about out here and waste money while others are desperately in need of it.

Strangely enough the weather isn't as hot as it should be in drought time. Only just reaches 100 degrees [38°C], never higher, so I guess we have a lot to be thankful for.

Len isn't home yet. No sense in him leaving there as we certainly need the money he earns. Although sometimes I wish there was a man here to help with some of the harder work.

There's hundreds of all kinds of birds around the house. The poor things are starving and come for any scraps of bread, peelings and seed and water. Our cats feast on them, judging by the feathers about, but still they come. Even wallabies and kangaroos, bandicoots, possums and rats in broad daylight. They are too hungry to be scared.

Brendan would have been three today. My eldest brother Tom also celebrates his 31st birthday today.

I'll get a Christmas parcel off to you, Fran, sometime next week as I'll have to get into Yeppoon for some food supplies then.

Well, I hope everything is going well over there at your house. Write soon.

Love,
Dulcie

Friday 19th November 1965

Dear Fran,

It's good to know someone, somewhere in this world is still having pleasant times. Your trip sounded wonderful and for the first time in my life I envy you the cold weather. I wouldn't care now if we had snow 20 feet [6 metres] deep - anything to escape this 100 degrees [38 °C] of heat, dust, and thirst. I've enclosed some newspaper cuttings. Need I say anything more about the drought?

CENTRAL QUEENSLAND IS DYING O
THIRST IN LONG DROUGHT

Central Queensland is dying of thirst as the drought, following seven poor seasons, strips the land of feed, evaporates the water, and bakes the waterholes.

Story by
BOB JOHNSON
Pictures by
BRIAN CHURCH

Terry has just passed his end of year exams and will be in Grade 2 next January. Four more weeks of school and then a break for Christmas. Christmas Day will pass like any other day for us this year. I can't see us celebrating anything other than the loss of everything we own.

Our Church of England minister called out last week and seemed shocked when I told him I am now an unbeliever. I cannot and will not believe there is a God after this. After the deaths of Karen and Brendan I accepted this minister's explanations for His reasons.

But I will not believe there is a God who has any reasons for letting innocent animals die in agony of thirst and hunger and sometimes bogged, just waiting hopelessly to die, while crows, hawks and dingos eat them alive. If this is done just to punish the people who own the stock, then it's a cruel rotten way to do it.

The Rev. McBlack took his departure still imploring me to have faith. Unless someone can explain it better than he did then Faith is a word of the past now as far as I'm concerned.

Oh Fran, what's the use. I can't even think straight enough to spell the words properly. To hell with life and everything else.

28th January 1966

Dear Fran,

Thank you so much for the lovely gifts you sent. All our friends have been fascinated by the tablecloth and key ring. I've been shopping and have found some little novelties to send you. Terry started school on January 24th in pouring rain. We've had 21 inches [53 cm] since Christmas. On Wednesday, the creek was flooded too high for the school bus to cross. So Len had to swim over and carry Terry back over to our side in the afternoon. Had I known the water was so high I wouldn't have sent him that morning. The rain has eased to scattered showers now so the creek was lower this morning.

Len decided against going away to NSW as we've been able to borrow £2000 from the bank to restock. The trouble is to find any stock for sale. We can't select the best breeds. Just have to take what is available. So now we have a mixture of Jersey, Hereford, Zebu, Illawarra, Santa Gertrudis and a few with a mixture of all breeds! However, we still have our own bulls that I hand fed last year so maybe we can breed a few decent things again.

We have to pay back £1000 by 31st December and the other £1000 the following year. Len will be going back to the cane in June to enable us to do this. We were planning to see if we could enlarge our family this year. Debts and all, we will have to go ahead or we will be too old soon. Terry is 7 now and it's 4 years in October since Brendan was born.

If our plans do become a fact, the only trouble will be Len is away for the last 6 months of the year. Still I think I could rely on Mum to mind Terry and the house pets for the week I'd be away and to baby-sit when I need to muster and dip, etc. Oh well, just keep your fingers crossed for me and we will see what happens!

Terry was thrilled to receive a letter from Ricky. Said he would write when he has time on the weekend. He doesn't have much spare time during the week as he has homework now to do after he gets home at 5 pm. And then I give him another try out on spellings, etc. before the bus calls at 7:30 am. Well, Fran, I must away and milk the old cow before Len and Terry arrive.

Lots of love,
Dulcie

16th February 1966

Dear Fran,

I can't find an easy way to tell you that we are once again sunk to the limit. Len's sister came home from hospital on February 1st and everyone seemed carefree and happy again to see her well. Then on Saturday 12th her husband phoned us. She had shot herself dead.

[Two paragraphs have been removed to protect surviving family members from a graphic description.]

All we can do now is make the children as happy as possible. The eldest boy Dennis, 18, is working at the Commonwealth Bank. Barbara will continue at college and James, 11, and Pat, 5, are at primary school and Len's mother has taken the baby aged 5 months.

Australia changed to decimal currency yesterday and I've posted an envelope for you with the first new cents stamp.

Lots of love,
Dulcie

7th March 1966

Dear Fran,

Received your letter and tape a few days ago. Terry was delighted with the boys' poems and enjoyed the recordings they played. At the time we made a tape to send you, our record player was broken down, but it's going again now and Terry has recorded some records for Ricky and Mark. But so far the tape isn't completed. I wanted Len to say a few words but I haven't been brave enough to speak to him about it yet.

Since his sister's death he is bad-tempered and shouts at Terry and me over the smallest thing. We had two of Violet's children here for 2 weeks but he seemed upset each time he came home and saw them so his parents took them.

I asked his mother to see if she could get Len to consult the doctor. Maybe a sedative would help him as he doesn't sleep well either. However, he raged at her too. So Terry and I just keep out of his way as much as possible.

I heard on the radio that North America is having a terrific blizzard. I do hope you are not in the path of it, Fran.

I went to Yeppoon today with Mum and Dad. The first time I've been to town for 4 or 5 weeks. Wasn't a very nice trip as we've had inches of rain and the road is all muddy and boggy. I drove down to our bottom boundary fence two days ago, to see if the cattle needed bone meal put out, and the car bogged on the way back. Terry and I walked the 3 miles [5 km] home to get the tractor to pull it out. Then the tractor bogged and it is still down there. Will have to wait till the rain stops and the ground gets hard now. Anyway there is green grass 2 feet [61 cm] high everywhere and the country looks really nice.

I'm sitting at the kitchen table watching the supper cook while I write this letter. Terry isn't home yet. The bus broke down yesterday afternoon and an old truck brought the kids home (all sitting out on the back in the pouring rain) at 5:45. Must have had another mishap today as its now 5:30 and no sign of the bus yet. Terry's raincoat is hanging in the bathroom cosy and dry where he left it last night so he will be dripping wet when he gets here.

Well, guess I'd better feed some animals and put them into their pens while I have time.

Lots of love,

Dulcie

PS We caught a little sea turtle on the beach a few weeks ago and it lived only a short time - so we had a man from Yeppoon stuff it. Terry thought Ricky and Mark might like it.

27th May 1966

Dear Fran,

Received your letter and the parcel of magazines. The papers arrived at a good time, me curled up in bed with flu, so I've been catching up on some reading. It's wonderful weather to lie in bed. We've had a few frosts and the days are chilly. I only get out to get breakfast and see Terry and Len off. Then feed the animals, ducks, etc. sweep the house, make the beds, wash the dishes and then back into bed till 4 o'clock, then prepare supper and feed animals again. Len and Terry both take their lunch with them.

We all had anti-influenza injections last year, but they don't seem much good. You mentioned measles vaccine in your letter. There was talk of it last year but the BMA [British Medical Association] wouldn't allow its use in Australia.

Ricky and Mark's photos are very good. They look so grown up compared to Terry. He is only just getting his front teeth and doesn't look very handsome just now!

We had a great time last Saturday night. It was Empire Day and 13 families gathered here to set off a fireworks display. The adults enjoyed it as much as the children. But gosh! You should see the lawn, it's littered with firecracker paper. I'll have a bonfire when I rake it up.

. . .

June 16th.

Well, Fran, I just didn't get around to ending this letter. We've been so busy. I recovered from the flu and have been extremely busy getting the work cleaned up so Len could leave for the north. He went on the plane Sunday night.

Terry and I and my parents are going to the Rockhampton Carnival tomorrow. I do hope the weather warms up a bit for it.

We had a visit from the people we picked fruit for in NSW today. It was lovely to meet them again. They drove 1700 miles [2736 km] up to see us and Len isn't home. They are staying in Yeppoon for 4 weeks so I shall be able to have a good talk to them later. They keep Brendan's grave in order for us at Griffith. I think this is very good of them.

Well, Fran, time is short and the school bus has just dropped Terry so I'll have to say cheerio.

Lots of love,
Dulcie

26th September 1966

Dear Fran,

Congratulations to Mark. His baseball team must be very good. I'm afraid baseball is not played in Australia but I imagine that it is very much the same as cricket. Am I right?

Terry's school just finished their annual inter-school sports. Terry's house won the shield again. Three years running now. They just made it this time by 3 points. I won the swimming again in the PTA [Parents Teachers Association] section. I've held the record since I was 14. However now the new pool is opened in Yeppoon the rest of the team will be able to practice more often so I'll probably miss out next year. I do my swimming in the cattle dams while the cattle look on with very interested expressions on their faces! Good day for swimming today.

The last week the weather has really warmed up - 101 [38°C]

today. The calf drop is well under way now with the warm weather. Every day there are more new ones to rear, mark and brand and give a vaccine to. I did 106 yesterday and only put in ½ a day today as I had to catch up with some housework.

Len's mum went home last week. Terry has a new pony I bought last week and he is anxious to try him out this weekend, so I'll have help with the cattle then and can catch up with the house-cleaning and baking. Just finished quite a pile of sewing - shirts and shorts for Ann's three boys.

Brian is thinking of selling their property and moving closer to town. Ann has never liked it out here. She was a city girl and finds it very lonely here. She can't drive and won't learn. She has no interest in gardening, can't sew or knit and has no interest in the property or stock. So I guess she would be better off and happier in town. Really can't see Brian getting an office job and being happy though.

I'm trying to listen to the radio while I write but the thunder storm keeps banging and making static. It's most annoying just when a song I especially like is being played. My favourites at the moment are "Angel of the Morning" "Kitty Can" and "Little Arrows". Will be going to Rockhampton next month some time and will shop for things to send you for Christmas.

Storm over the land

Is there anything any member of the family would especially

like, Fran? The macadamia nuts will be as scarce as they were last year I'm afraid. The horses eat them all off the trees as high up as they can reach. Just as well they like them green - they sure wouldn't be able to chew the ripe ones up!

Father Clarke's [Len's father] friend came out from USA and had a good trip over by plane and returned last week. I only got to see him once for about ½ an hour. I always meant to make time to talk to him again but the days just flew and before I knew it, it was time for him to go. He is very nice, not as old as I thought he would be.

He went up to see Len and they of course had a good time together. Len was 15 when he last met him. Anyway, he will be retiring from his job in 32 months and is coming back to live here. So guess I'll have to wait till then to get to know him.

Well, Fran, the school bus will soon be in and I'll have to meet Terry in the car as it's raining quite heavily now. The rain mixed with the bangs and lightning flashes has really ruined my radio program.

Write soon and hope you are all well.

Love,

Dulcie

8th November 1966

Dear Fran,

Well, I spent a day in town yesterday and finished all my Christmas shopping. It's so much easier to do it before Terry finishes school. I can hurry through the stores without worrying about him getting lost.

It's very stormy looking today and hot enough for a 102 degrees [39°C]. We could do with 4 inches [10 cm] of rain too.

Terry and I had to take the tractor 5 miles [8 km] down to the paddock to pull a cow out of the creek last Friday afternoon. She had 2 new calves sucking her and she was very weak. Poor old thing, we had to shoot her and the calves. One of the calves she adopted from another dead cow. I hated killing the calves but they would have tagged onto other cows and we'd lose them too.

How's Ricky's guitar lessons going? He is a good age to start learning. Tell him to practice every spare minute he has and it won't be long before he is perfect. Terry had difficulties with the guitar, his fingers become sore and blistered so he has been learning piano for some time now.

You wrote that Mark asked why no one gathers around and has singsongs any more. Well, here we just have to if we haven't any amusement. There is no TV and it's too far to go to town very often. So we all gather at different homes and "state" a concert now and again.

Most of our instruments are easy to carry about and if the home doesn't have a piano, well, we do without it and make enough noise to disguise the fact. Our guitars have battery powered amplifiers as there is no electricity.

No, Fran, Tom doesn't race his car. He says he is too old. He turned 32 on October 25th.

Did I tell you Len's younger sister was expecting triplets? Well, she only had twin boys after all. Both big babies 6 pounds 10 ounces [3 kg] each. She named them John and Mark.

My brother's wife, Ann, also had another son, 7 pounds 4 ounces [3.3 kg]. They were very disappointed because it wasn't a girl. Still, he's a lovely little fellow. Their twin boys are just 17 months old so Ann will have her hands full for awhile. Gosh, this looks bad for us with twins on both sides of the family.

Last week there was a Square Dancing and Country Music film showing in Rockhampton. The title "Country Music on Broadway". A shocking long way to go to see a film I know but I just couldn't resist it. It was lovely! The square dancing group were called the "Stony Mountain Cloggers". Gee, I thought they were great.

[https://www.youtube.com/watch?v=hKkEC7O8_2E]

Some of the singers were: Furlin Huskey, Bill Anderson, Hank Williams (Senior and Junior) Hank Snow and Andy Williams. The other feature was about a plant in Detroit that crushes old car bodies up and melts them down into steel plate again. Have you seen this place, Fran? Heck, I think it's a clever idea.

Well, in closing this hasty scribble I must thank you for the books. I read the American Presidential one and enjoyed it very much. Terry also was very interested.

I sent you a parcel and included a woman's paper with an article in it about President Johnson's visit. We heard a radio broadcast on his arrival at Canberra and the speech he made. He has quite a good sense of humour, hasn't he?

Well, I must close and get some work done, Fran.

So lots of love,

Dulcie

January 1967

Dear Fran,

Well, what a busy and hot old time we've had since 2nd December. Len finished his cane cut and came home near the end of November and we had two hectic weeks mustering and dipping. When Terry's school closed for the 6 weeks summer holidays, we packed up and took him for a trip to inspect the big copper mine at Mt. Morgan. We had a wonderful time, but gosh it was hot! We have some photos, etc. to send you later.

We came back two weeks before Christmas and Len was taken ill with a kidney complaint. With the temp still up to 109 [43°C] day and night, Terry and I managed to hold the fort again and also kill the poultry, etc. and prepare the Christmas goodies. But by the time Len was well, it was 2 days off Christmas and then we were all too worn out to enjoy ourselves. There's still no change in the weather. This summer is the longest and hottest since 1961. However, I guess we will live through it.

Your package arrived in perfect order and what a thrill we got unpacking it. We all adored the racing car and the little soap monkey! When it grew fur it attracted all our neighbours. No one had ever seen such a thing happen. Gosh, if only we could live in USA for awhile! The tin of crackers was delicious too.

Most of all I liked the painting set. Terry gave them to me to do. How I've enjoyed every minute painting. I could hardly drag myself away to do the work. Now they are finished they really look beautiful. Have you tried them, Fran? If they are not expensive I would dearly love the ones I've enclosed, Fran. Forgive me for being greedy enough to ask you. Is there anything you would like us to send you in return? Please just forget your manners, like I have, and ask for whatever you'd like. We can get the oil paints here but not the numbered sketches to paint. So if you can just get them without the paint as it leaks on to the painting on the way over.

We went to Rockhampton to the annual Tropical Bull Sale last Monday and bought ourselves a few new ¾ Brahman Bulls. We all got terrifically sunburnt too. One thing good about this breed of cattle though, hot weather doesn't worry them at all.

Well, Fran, I must away now and much as I hate going outside, I must work. Thank you once again for the lovely parcel.

Love,
Dulcie

14th February 1967

Dear Fran,

Although the heat is terrific, I don't think I'd like all your snow. I'd love to see a little bit but really can't stand the temp below 70 degrees [21°C]. Tasmania, our most southern state, has had terrific heat and the worst fires in Australia's history. Over 50 people dead and hundreds of homes destroyed.

We had 6 inches [15 cm] of rain in 2 hours last week from a thunder storm. Gosh, the roads were boggy. I imagine your snow slush was something like it. I drove up to Rockhampton to get six teeth extracted. I had to fit chains to the back tyres and it took me 3 hours to get there.

Didn't think I'd make it back home in time to meet the school bus so I telephoned Mum to collect Terry. Just as well as I ran into a string of bogged cars with a council grader pulling them out. Didn't get home till 8 o'clock that night and by then the numbness had worn off my mouth and it was a bit painful.

Went out on the horse next morning to get the cattle on to high ground as they get foot rot in the mud. By that night I felt a bit worse so next morning drove back through the mud to the dentist and had to get antibiotics and some anti-pain tablets. Doesn't feel too bad now.

Just hope the loss of these teeth are worth it as they were quite sound. But for 18 months I've had abscesses continually in both ears that the doctors couldn't seem to clean up. So they decided 3 back teeth each side of the lower jaw be removed to see if that clears up the trouble. Personally I think a good long sleep might cure everything. Just don't seem to get time to sleep any longer than 5 or 6 hours out of every 24.

Len went away 3 weeks ago with two of his friends on a tour of the southern States. They'll be away till the middle of April. Gee, how I envy them the lovely time they are having.

I don't know what Len is going to say when he reads my next letter. I got fed up with some of the cattle that were too wild and I rounded up 53 of them and sent them to the sale. Just about killed my horse and myself galloping after those scrubbers. There's only one bad one now, a black Brahman bull. He charges the horses and I have to be quick off the mark to dodge him. Next time I get him in I'll dehorn the thing and he won't be so dangerous.

We bought the 53 steers a year ago for $42 a head and sold them for $92 so didn't do too badly. Len had planned on keeping them for 2 years but he doesn't have to work the wild things.

In my spare(?) time I'm putting in a water-lily fish pond in the garden. It is 11 feet x 8 feet [3.4 x 2.4 metres] and 3 feet deep [91 cm]. I have nearly finished digging the hole (hard-going, too) and then have to cement it and plant up the edges. Should be nice if I ever get it done. Terry helps dig and shovel when he comes home from school. Wish I had a few more Terrys! Perhaps you could send Ricky and Mark over to work for me!

Well, Fran, I've got cattle yarded waiting to be dipped so guess I'll have to get a move on.

Lots of love,
Dulcie

18th June 1967

Dear Fran,

As usual, will you forgive me for taking so long to write? Weeks ago I received the parcel and birthday card and two letters from you. Thank you very much for all of them. Although I don't write very often, I love to hear from you.

I've been frantically busy ever since Len left at the end of January. He only got back two weeks ago and ever since then we've been flood-bound. Can't cross the two bridges on the road to

Yeppoon. One is still 4 feet 5 inches [137 cm] over the bridge and the other 3 feet [91 cm]. So Terry hasn't been able to go to school. He was lucky to get home. The first day I noticed the creek rising I went into Yeppoon and got him at lunch time. Just got home as the water was washing the decking.

We have been busy getting the stock to high ground and the weaker ones into shelter. So far we have had 15 inches [38 cm] of rain and it shows no sign of letting up yet. So plenty of time to write a letter as it may not get posted for another few days. Just as well we have enough food, etc. stocked up. Only hope no one gets sick now.

While Len was away, we had an outbreak of foot-rot and botulism in the cattle. I had to get all the affected ones into one paddock and yard them every day and give them injections. Boy, what a job! One week I had 95 sick ones. Took me all day to cope with them. For two weeks running there just wasn't time to sit down to eat. So I ate on the move.

To top it all off at the same time the engine on No. 2 bore broke down. Sat up till 3 o'clock in the morning with the headlights of the tractor to fix it.

Next day the truck played up. The generator wanted new brushes, etc. so I did that next night. Got in it next morning to cart the lucern down and the starter motor wouldn't work. Like all stupid Fords it has no crank handle so I towed it with the tractor while Terry drove it and started it.

That night found me in the shed with the tractor lights on putting new brushes and re-bundling the fields on that. Was rather fed up with working in the half-dark by then. So went up to Rockhampton next day and came back with a home electricity plant. Took 2 and ½ days to wire the house, with Terry's help at night, and then rigged up the engine and everything and thought we'd have lights. Very funny, because I couldn't crank the big diesel engine over.

So had a starter motor sent down next day and fixed up an electric start on it. Gee, Fran, I wish you could see our house now! Electric lights in every room plus power points, I even have an electric iron. We can also run TV off it. So later on we'll have a set.

These home power units are becoming very popular in the country where there is never likely to be town power. What's more it costs very little a week to have such a luxury. To use the lights, there's no need to start the engine as the 12 batteries of 12 volts each are charged up enough to keep them bright. But the iron, TV, etc have to have the engine running to work. Of course we can't run as many things as the town supply of 240 volts can but still, it's lovely. The whole thing only cost $1067. Saved a bit by installing it and wiring the house myself.

I didn't let Len know about it. I kept it as a surprise for him when he came home. You should have seen his face when I just walked into the house and flicked a switch and the lights came on! Now we can fix things in the shed at night with a decent light.

Terry is quite fascinated by it and leaves his light on when he's gone to bed. All he wants now is TV so after we sell the next lot of stock in December we will get a set for sure.

While I was busy with all the breakdowns and sick cattle, our neighbour, a few miles away, got mumps and had to go to the hospital. His wife (a useless type of woman) sent one of the kiddies over on his pony to see if I would go over to muster his cattle and dip them and drive her into town to see him at the hospital.

I did all his cattle, fixed up the windmill on the house bore and by then was in a bad mood. So I told her to get into their new car and learn to drive it or get on a horse and learn to ride it and then take a course in mechanics.

It's really amazing how a city type hopes to live in the country. All country women are as capable as men and can take over the properties, and run them when their men folks are away. So she sure has a lot to learn.

Well, Fran, it's lunch time, so I guess I'd better close and feed the family.

Lots of love,
Dulcie

—✳——✳——✳—

Saturday 29th July 1967

Dear Fran,

I've been so worried about you all since I've heard about the racial trouble in Detroit. People killed, injured and buildings wrecked. Fran, I do hope you and your family were unharmed. We've never had any riots in Australia, but I think I can understand what a terrible time people must have during such trouble. I just hope all your family and possessions were untouched.

Len went back cane-cutting again on June 30th. He wasn't going to go but he thought he may as well get as much money as possible, before he got too old. Then he can settle down and tackle his own place in comfort. Sometimes I wish he'd get old quickly so I could have him here all the time. I wonder what will happen if I feel too old to carry on here without him. Sometimes I feel so tired and with just Terry for company, it gets a bit lonely. However I know Len is doing this for our sakes, so I mustn't dwell on self-pity.

We've had a very poor winter this year (thank heavens)! Just a few light frosty mornings and lovely hot days. The rain has been welcome and unusual for this time of the year. The animals are all looking wonderful and the garden is glorious. Nothing got frosted this year.

We had a wonderful surprise a few weeks ago. The Sub-Normal Children's Association are having a fund raising campaign to build a new centre in Brisbane and a four-hour concert is to be held at the Town Hall in Rockhampton. Three of Queensland's recording stars will be singing (Slim Dusty and Chad Morgan, the other one I can't remember off-hand) and Tom, the boys and myself have been asked to appear. We have been allotted 1 hour of the time.

Needless to say we are very thrilled and we will have to busy ourselves practicing for the big night on August 5th. Maybe I can get someone to catch a few of the numbers on tape for you.

Thirty-eight baby ducklings hatched last week and Terry is doing a wonderful job looking after them. He always tends one batch until the next comes out then he takes the new ones. Things only appeal to him when they are very small! He added another animal to his private zoo a few weeks ago. Dad caught him a small bandicoot.

I wonder what's going to become of his wallabies, emus, turtles and other things when he grows up and leaves home!

Fran, I forgot to put our new address on the first page. The post office has given us a Mail Service number and post code, so now our address is M.S. 142 Yeppoon 4703. Much easier to spell than the old one.

Well, Fran, I must away to work. Please let me know how you all are soon.

Love,
Dulcie

12th December 1967

Dear Fran,

Yesterday was one of those days when nothing goes right. The temp was 104 [40°C] inside the house when I came home from fixing a fence. My head ached and sunburn stung when I had a bath and altogether I felt annoyed with the whole day. After tea my parents came and Mum had taken delivery of your parcel from the transport driver.

How I cheered up! The salt and pepper shakers are lovely and the sachet of cream was so nice. I rubbed some on my sunburnt face, smelt good and felt good. We had loads of fun with the magic ball. Terry set himself up as a fortune teller and the answers to some questions we asked were really good! Many thanks indeed, Fran, it made a good finish to a bad day.

This summer is a beauty. Most days have been well over 100 [38°C] inside. Wish we had air-conditioning. One thunderstorm last week gave us 4 inches [10 cm] of rain, so the heat hasn't affected the fodder too bad and water is plentiful too. Len will be home on 15th December so then we will have busy days until all the branding, dehorning, castration, etc. is done. Terry starts his holidays on 15th December and has 6 weeks off until January 22nd. He is a good help at the stock-yards, fetches and carries for us and stops and starts the engine, etc.

I plan on baking the Christmas cake in two days time. Might be cooler to do it at night. Terry wanted a microscope and a new record player this year. Bought both when I went to Rockhampton last week as I may not get there again before Christmas.

Well, Fran, the washing is dry now so I must bring it in and make the beds. Many thanks again for the parcel and Merry Christmas to all.

Lots of love,
Dulcie

5th January 1968

Dear Fran,

Well, the holidays are over now and it's back to work for most people. What a Christmas! The really hot weather started near the end of November and reached a peak on Christmas day. I don't think many people in the state really enjoyed the day. The temp inside our house was 110 [43°C] and the humidity at night 93 percent.

Brisbane has a normal temp of 88 [31°C] but reached 101 [38°C]. Some western towns reported 115 [46°C] and over. New Year's day was the same but yesterday a cool change arrived and now it's only 98 degrees [37°C]. This is the longest heat wave since 1911. On Boxing Day we went to the beach but the shark signals were hoisted and the water was deserted.

We've had thunderstorms every day but no rain, just terrific lightning and thunder. Some places have had quite a few cattle struck with lightning, so we insured the last Brahman Bull we bought. If he gets killed at least we'll get some of our money back.

Len and I have been erecting a new fence for the last week, in between spells under shady trees. It is 1 and ½ miles long with 4 barbed strands. Gosh, it's hot work!

Terry's old collie bitch had 7 pups on Christmas day. She is 9 years old so we didn't let her keep any. Terry didn't like them because they were black like their father, just as well.

At present Australia is without a prime minister. Mr Holt disappeared a few weeks ago while swimming. It is generally thought he was taken by a shark. There had been two previous shark attacks at the same beach and the victims' bodies were never found. It doesn't appear Mr Holt's body will be found either after all this time.

Well, Fran, Len has finished welding something or other on Terry's bike and is now looking for tea so I must away.

Hope your Christmas was nice and snowy. One day I hope to see snow before I get too old to make a snowman.

Lots of Love,
Dulcie

20th January 1968

Dear Fran,

Your letter arrived only yesterday but I'm answering early as I have some spare time.

I had some trouble yarding three bulls last week. I was riding a young flighty horse and it threw me twice. I gave it a good belting and got mounted again and hit the dust for the third time.

Next day my back pained like mad. I put up with it for 5 days and went to the doctor. Just bruised and jarred so I'm having a day or two of rest. Will be able to catch up on all the letter writing as there sure won't be time later on.

The weather is lovely and warm now during the days, around the 80s [27°C]. Nights are still a little cold at mostly 45 to 50 [7 - 10°C] and one has to wear a coat in the early part of the morning.

I can understand Dick enjoying his recliner chair. When my

grandparents (Dad's people) came out from England in 1897, they brought two recliner chairs with them.

The chairs were passed on to Mum and Dad after the old couple's death. When Terry was born, Dad gave me one of the old chairs and although it's very old-fashioned, with funny carved squiggles all over it, it is very comfortable and many are the nights I have fell asleep in it.

Yes, Fran, the concert went off with a bang and we had a wonderful time. Radio 1000 broadcast it state-wide and as my parents didn't go, they were able to tape a section of it from the radio. So, as soon as I can, I'll mail it.

How is your kitten doing? I like cats much better than dogs. At one time we had five cats but one or two died from snake bites and the others got run over so now we've only got one old ginger cat.

He seems to lead a charmed life. Once when I backed the car out of the shed, he got his back legs run over. Then Len ran over him with the tractor once and a black snake bit him early this year. However, he is still going strong although he has plenty of scars, two crooked legs and a bent tail.

Terry's old collie had seven pups a month ago. I killed them all as Collie is nearly nine years old now and with pups to feed she couldn't pick up in health. She has only seven teeth left and has to be fed on soft food.

She is the oldest dog we have and the other four working dogs are blue heelers. We use these for driving cattle. They work very much like sheep dogs only instead of barking they run quietly and bite the legs of any cattle that get out of line.

A good heeler can do the work of two riders. Of course it takes time to train a young dog but it soon learns from the older dogs. Terry is reading this letter as I write and he said to tell Ricky and Mark that in the grain shed there are 23 cats - he counted them yesterday!

I don't count these as pets because they are not allowed to be brought to the house, they are strictly working cats. Their job is to keep the mice and rats out of the stock feed. They only get ¾ gallon of milk each day and have to catch anything else they want to eat.

Well, Fran, I guess we need some lunch so I'll away for now.
Lots of love,
Dulcie

--- ✳ --- ✳ --- ✳ ---

10th February 1968

Dear Fran,

Last week we were invited to do another show with some recording artists to raise funds for charity. This is a tape Len took while sitting in the audience. Hence the loud yells. He tried to cut most of it out. Anyway, I hope you can hear the tunes okay.

We started off with Slim Dusty a leading recording artist and holder of two gold records. All together doing "Along the Road to Gundagai" and "I'm Going Back to Yarrawonga".

Next he sang a "Fire of Gidgee Coal". Then a portion of Tom doing "Lofty" and "Back Street Affair".

Tom was troubled with his amplifier all night. It insisted on making crackling noises. Been doing this for some time now. I guess he should discard it.

Next Slim Dusty again with "Queensland State So Fair" and "Ace of Hearts". A pity Len didn't record all of that number as I like it very much. "In the Dog House Now" is another number by Tom.

Next, our own group doing "Guitar Boogie".

Then Rick Clearly and I with a duet and violin backing, "Let's Grow Old Together". Last for this side is Dusty Rankin doing "Little Blue Eyes".

On side 2, I kicked off with a solo "I'll Be All Smiles Tonight". Then funny man Chad Morgan with "Two Up". Dusty Rankin again with "The Drifting Stockman". Tom still with amplifier trouble doing "Sunshine My Side of the Street". Rick and I with an encore to do "Let's Grow Old Together" again. Slim Dusty with "Sesias Jace" and, to close, me doing a repeat of "I'll be all Smiles Tonight".

Hearing ourselves against the professionals just shows that we sure aren't much good. Anyway we helped make up a show and the money came rolling in for a good cause.

Well, Fran, hope you think the tape is worth wasting the batteries over.

Lots of love,

Dulcie

14th April 1968

Dear Fran,

Today is Easter Sunday so we are having an extra long lunch break before we go back to branding and dehorning. Two jobs I hate most. The hot brand may not hurt for long but when the horns are removed, just like teeth, gosh! I'm glad I'm not a cow.

Since February there just hasn't been a spare moment. Len went interstate with some friends on 9th February. Two days later the wet season started and this time it was extra wet. In 3 weeks we had 63 inches [160 cm] of rain. We were cut off on all roads and the Army helicopters at the Shoalwater Base, which joins our property, kept in contact with us in case we needed anything.

Terry couldn't go to school and he moped about trying to find something to do. I took all the stock to higher ground after the first of the rain. Some places were so flooded I had to get off the horse and swim with it. Then we had an outbreak of ephemeral fever in the cattle which meant they had to be hand-fed and watered where they lay. If you try to walk them they die.

I lost count of the times the truck bogged with loads of feed on. Terry came in handy then. He managed the truck while I towed it out with the crawler. Putting feed and buckets of water under each animal's nose twice a day for 10 days - 280 of them, too - we just tumbled into bed around midnight each night.

All this time the phone was out and the roads out and Len couldn't be contacted. As soon as the animals were okay Len's father had a heart attack. I nursed him for 4 days waiting for a helicopter to come over to signal it down. They were the worst 4 days and nights I've ever known.

He lives in another house on our place, ½ mile from our house. I went to see him one evening and found him unable to speak properly and hardly able to walk. Terry and I got him into the truck and brought him home. I don't know much about medicine and thought he would die before we got help.

However on the 5th day a copter came over the house and I put Terry on the roof to wave a sheet. It came down and took the old chap to hospital. He came home 12 days ago and has been staying with us.

He and his wife parted many years ago. Eight days ago my mother also had a heart attack. She is still in hospital but progressing alright. Len came home 6 days ago and we are busy once more. We took Good Friday off and went fishing, didn't do much good as the fresh water run off had killed most of the crabs and oysters. Anyway, we had a day out.

I've just found your last letter, looked it up to see how long it was since I'd wrote you a letter. You mentioned square dancing. I believe a fair bit of it is done in the southern states but in Queensland it appeared to die out in 1953-54. I remember doing this dance when I was still in high school - it was very popular then and I loved the full skirted frocks. Seems a pity it's not done here now.

How are you going with the income tax business? Yes, Fran, we pay tax too, 10 cents in every dollar we earn. Doesn't allow anyone to get rich. I do all the book-keeping and tax returns. Every month my big headache begins when it's time to pay the accounts and enter it in the books. Of course we don't pay tax on the gross income just what is left after we deduct farming expenses.

For instance we may have a gross income of $8,000 but fodder, fuel, machinery, fencing requirements, etc. may amount to $5000 So we are taxed on what is left. We can claim deductions for everything put into or onto the land but not living expenses or personal things. The cost of Terry's schooling is deductible - books, fees and uniforms, etc.

Most of the articles I've seen about American schools, the children appear to wear what they like. Is this really so, Fran? Here, each school, private or public, has its own uniform in the school colours. Terry's is grey and blue which means he must wear grey trousers and a shirt trimmed with a blue band on the sleeves. Socks are grey with blue stripe at the top. Grey and blue striped tie and grey hat with the school brand and motto. The girls have grey frocks with sleeves trimmed with blue and grey, stockings and tie. They look very neat and each school is proud of its colours.

Well, Fran, I've cut myself a bit short of time to do the other things I planned to do this lunch time. I must get the washing soaked in to do tonight and make up the extra beds for two of Terry's playmates. They are coming late this evening to stay till Monday night. Then I must leave everything in order for Len to baby sit while I go to Rockhampton to visit Mum tonight (if possible after I've done the washing).

Well, I must away and do these things and then back to work or Len will be growling about women who waste time, a favourite growl.

Lots of love, and write often. I love hearing from you even though I don't write often myself.

Dulcie

PS Enclosed some stamps for the boys. Terry has the collecting bug also and thought Ricky and Mark would like these.

Tuesday 23rd April 1968

Dear Fran,

Many thanks for the lovely birthday card. It arrived on Monday and until then no one, not even myself, thought of it being my birthday the day before. We had a good excuse - tiredness.

On Saturday the school had its second Marathon Walk to raise funds for a swimming pool, the cost of which is $32,000. The government refused to build a pool but promised to give $1 for every $1 raised by Yeppoon and Districts with a population of 3,000 people. At the beginning this looked an impossible task and I think the government thought we would never be able to raise $16,000.

We thought up this idea of human race-horses, the idea being everyone who wanted to walk should get as many people as possible to sponsor him at so much per mile. Generally most people sponsored from 1 cent to 10 cents per mile. We went as far as Rockhampton for sponsors.

Terry walked 36 miles [58 km] this year and raised $30.36. Last year's walk he did only 30 miles [48 km] and raised $36.00. We set out at six o'clock in the morning and only had till six in the evening to walk. The police were very good and kept the traffic at a slow pace all the way. At each mile peg an adult manned a checkpoint where you could pull out of the walk if you chose and a pick-up car would collect all the "dropouts" and return them to the starting point.

When Terry dropped out at 36 miles, I continued on and reached "home" at 5 minutes to six so completing the 40 mile [64 km] course with just 5 minutes to spare. I was backed for 48 cents per mile, so only raised $19.20 after all that walking!

However, some of the children walked the whole distance with only 10 cents per mile given. Oh well, we are only $5000 short of our target now, so another walk is planned later this year. One thing, Yeppoon people can be really proud of the pool they earned the money for.

Mark and Ricky are sure growing up fast, Fran. Terry loved the style of their hair-cuts. Here they have to stick to school regulation cuts, short back and sides sort of thing, like the Army.

I've just finished hanging out the washing and trying to bake bread and cakes while writing and listening to the radio. Len and Terry have gone to bed. The song "Memories of Honey" by Bobby Goldsboro is my favourite at the moment. In fact I'm crazy about it. I think it's quite beautiful although a little sad.

I went in to see Mum yesterday evening - she won't be home for maybe six weeks so the doctor says.

Well, Fran, maybe if I stop writing I'll finish the work quicker and get to bed.

Lots of love and thanks again for the card,
Dulcie

9th August 1968

Dear Fran,

It must be months since I wrote you and so much has happened in that time. The death of Mr. Kennedy [Robert Kennedy] was a terrible thing. I was hoping he would be your next president.

At the end of May, Terry was admitted to hospital with bronchial pneumonia. He was there for 4 weeks. One week after I brought him home he had a relapse and was back in again, a very sick boy, for another 5 weeks. I brought him home again a couple of weeks ago. He won't be able to return to school until the end of this month.

He has had bronchitis ever since he was about 9 months old and every winter gets influenza and I always watch him carefully. However, this time he said he wasn't feeling too ill and wanted to go to school to finish his first term exam. He finished it okay, got good marks too. English 98%, Social Studies 99%, Maths 84%, other subjects 92%. How he managed I don't know because that very weekend he was terribly ill and put straight into hospital. When I showed him his exam results, he said he should have done better! Some people are never satisfied.

Len left in mid-June to go back to the cane again. He came down to see Terry during his second stay in hospital but hasn't been back since. We need a new car, the old one has just about parted from us. So we have to find $4,000 to buy another. Len won't borrow from the bank or use time purchase so he is working to earn it.

This time we are going to buy a Valiant. Our truck, car and tractors are all Ford and have given us no end of trouble, so I think it's time to leave that make. No one seems to have a good word to say about Ford lately. The Ford Falcon gave everyone trouble. Mainly the gear box and differential appeared too weak for the car. Maybe our rough roads don't suit.

I've been kept pretty busy here lately. I don't know if the USA is interested in our tick problem, so maybe you haven't heard, but Queensland cattle ticks are getting rather hard to kill and we now have what is termed resistant ticks in many areas. Any property found with them on is quarantined by the Department of Primary Industries. Also the properties adjoining, as in our case one of our neighbours has the resistant ticks, so we are also under quarantine.

Every ten days I have to muster and yard the cattle and dip them with chemicals the DPI are experimenting with. No stock, cattle, horses, dogs, etc. can be moved off the place and no plants soil or anything else in which ticks might be present. It means we can't sell cattle for maybe 6 months or so until they've cleared our neighbour. It makes a lot of work dipping so often.

Usually we dip only every 7 weeks. With Terry sick it made things awkward but Len's mother came to my rescue and is staying with us so she minds Terry and helps with the housework. Heck! I'll miss her when she goes home.

I probably told you before that she and Len's father parted many years ago, long before I met Len. They are Catholics so are not divorced. Mother has a cattle property of her own and is quite well off. Father lives in the old home on our place. Mother has a manager to run her place and travels about a fair bit. She doesn't visit us very often because of her husband being on the place. Funny, they are both very nice people and yet can't stand the sight of each other.

Both of Len's sisters, the one now dead and Margaret, were baptised in the parents' faith but Len was brought up Church of England. Seems a funny thing to have done and whenever we have asked the parents why they did this, they both say, "We had our reasons" and that's the end of the subject. Oh well, suits me, makes Len and I the same faith.

The days are warming up nicely again. Was 80 degrees [27°C]

yesterday, a little cooler today. How I love to see winter take off! Fitted in a bit of gardening last week. First time I've replanted anything since the 1964, '65 drought. Kind of lost interest then when lots of things died. Probably have another dry year now that I planted up again! Cheerful, aren't I!

I put in one dozen new roses and wish I could have hundreds, I love roses. Also planted up the orchard again. Grapes, oranges, lemons, custard apples, mulberries, bananas, mandarins, pawpaws, passion fruit, avocados, grapefruit and a few other things. Missed our fruit last year. So here's to a big crop next year.

Well, Fran, have a happy birthday and celebrate somewhere nice.

Love,

Dulcie

PS I just remembered. A man from New York, I think, he was staying with the Clarkes during his Army service out here during the last war, is coming to stay with Len's father for a few weeks. He gets here August 28th. We'll tell you about him next letter. Maybe he can visit you when he goes back and tell you about us.

5th December 1968

Dear Fran,

Guess you are having some fun in the snow now. Every time I think of you having sled rides and making snowmen and skating I turn green with envy. Not that I like cold weather but I'd just love to see snow.

Summer got off to a good start here. The temp has varied between 102 to 104 [39 to 40°C] the past month. Every second day or so a storm comes roaring and banging. Last Monday we had a really terrific one - blew down trees, unroofed sheds and some houses (not ours, thank heaven). The school bus didn't arrive until 6:30 that night. The road was blocked with fallen trees.

It is raining at the moment and the sky is lit with lightning. Our close neighbour, a German woman, is terrified of storms and when her husband is not home she runs the 1 and ½ miles to stay with me. At the moment both her and her 16 year old daughter are huddled in the kitchen playing games with Terry. I had some bookwork to do in the office so I've also taken the opportunity to write a couple of letters while they finish their game. The noise of thunder reminds the poor thing of the bombing raids over Germany during the last war. She is a nice woman and would do anything to help anyone.

Remember me telling you about the little kitten Terry had? The thing has developed into a man-eating tiger! When he is on the floor, he bites feet and legs. When he's picked up he bites arms, hands and even our faces. If this is his way of showing thanks for being saved I don't like it.

We went into Yeppoon last Saturday night to the movies. A double feature, one was a cowboy film. Terry loves these. The only thing I like about them are the lovely cactus plants growing everywhere. I especially like how big they grow. If ever I get to USA, Fran, the first thing I'll do is send back a big crate full of cactus. I have a fair cactus garden now but nothing like those American ones.

Well, I must rejoin the others as their game is over now and as the storm shows no sign of abating, I'll have to prepare beds for the guests.

Merry Christmas, Fran, to you and all your family and have a good time.

Love,
Dulcie

PART III

1969 - 1973

9th May 1969

Dear Fran,

For the first time in months I have a few minutes spare. First of all have I thanked you for the Christmas parcel? What manners I have! Also Terry's birthday card and mine. And anything else I've neglected to thank you for.

We are terribly overworked here. I thought we worked hard before but now we do twenty hours a day. All the western half of Queensland is still drought-stricken and the State Government has ruled that any grazier with grass land must take the cattle from drought areas. Three hundred head of cattle were brought to us and we are forced to care for them until the owners are able to take them back after rain.

They were brought here at the end of November last and look like being here for another year at least. Together, with our more than 400, it makes hard work for Len and myself. The government pays us $120 per week for keeping them. The big Army training area at Shoalwater Bay near us is also being used to feed stock.

There are 44,000 head of cattle there at the moment. Being a tick-free area the men there haven't much work to do though.

Sure messes things up. We have done fifteen miles of fencing since December and put in three dams and one bore for extra water. All this at our own expense to house other folks' cattle. For their sake and ours I hope rain falls in the west before too long.

Had a broken foot and two toes in February. A bull jumped the gate, knocked me over and jumped on my foot. A half-ton [508 kg] bull sure is heavy! Slowed me down for a few weeks but is okay now.

Terry had his share of trouble too. His horse tripped and fell and Terry got a few nasty scratches and bruises. He didn't think to check his horse for injuries and remounted the poor thing. He came galloping up behind some wild steers and the horse went down again. Len gave Terry a sound scolding for riding an injured horse and packed Terry and the horse off home, both limping. They are both recovered now, thank heavens.

We had an outing last weekend, the first time we've been out since Christmas. A friend's son celebrated his 21st birthday. Was a wonderful party and we really enjoyed ourselves even though it was hard to get out of bed next morning.

Well, Fran, I must catch the mail transport with this letter so excuse the shortness and write soon. I love getting your letters and wish I could manage to write to you more often.

Love from,
Dulcie

23rd August 1969

Dear Fran,

Winter appears to have left us, thank heavens, and the days and nights are becoming lovely again. We still have all the cattle on drought relief with no sign of rain for the western areas.

Len, Terry and Len's father went out through the drought areas last week and spent a couple of days digging for sapphires on the gem fields. Terry found one and is quite pleased with himself. It's back to school again tomorrow after 2 weeks mid-term vacation.

Remember me telling you about the little kitten Terry brought home last year, Fran? Somewhere along the way his name got changed to "Sugarplum" and he is now a full grown cat. Just now he brought his "catch" in to show me and as a result there are feathers all over the room. He loves me to admire him when he has caught something. One night he brought in a possum - still alive - and let it go on the bed.

Len is putting down a bore for more water. It is 58 feet deep [17.7 metres] and seems to have quite a good supply although it is rather salty, 360 grams to the gallon. Still it should be good for cattle.

Well, Fran, like time, news is scarce so have a happy birthday, do something nice to celebrate and write and tell me about it.

Love,
Dulcie

27th November 1969

Dear Fran,

I've been thinking of you so much since I received your last letter. Somehow, I feel that something is wrong. You don't seem to be your usual cheerful self. I hope it's nothing wrong in the family, Fran. If it is just the winter getting you down, come over and share our summer. It's only just started but the temps have been over 100 [38°C] for days now.

Len and I have been felling timber - Len carrying a chainsaw about all day - but the heat has reduced me to an axe. Even that is hard enough to swing all day. Had quite a good storm 2 days ago which yielded 160 points of rain. [One point is 0.254 mm or 0.01 inches.] Much needed too as the feed quickly burns off in the heat. Our drought cattle are still with us and look as if they are here to stay. Two Brahman cows died calving last week and I have the calves here to feed. I start them off sucking my finger in a bucket of milk until they learn to drink. One feeds quite good but the other bites.

Posted off a Christmas parcel for you last week. So hard to find anything unusual. The little koala for you is made of kangaroo skin, the kind known as Blue, hence the blue fur. Terry selected the 'roo skin caps for the boys and Dick. The large colourful map you might like to hang in the basement. Len suggested the Australian beer, etc. for Dick to celebrate with. Hope you have a good time!

My eldest brother Tom was married on 25th October, his 35th birthday. His bride looked so nice. A small girl always does, I think. Me and my skinny 5 feet 6 inches [168 cm], I look and sometimes feel ungainly!

Terry is doing his final year exam this week and starts 6 weeks holidays on 14th December. He is now a member of the Yeppoon Swimming Club and hopes one day to take my title from me which I still hold for the 100 metres overarm. The club meets every Wednesday night for competitive racing and although it's tiring, I enjoy the cool off.

Well, Fran, I've guests to dinner tonight and although I finished work early to come home and prepare I'm afraid I've not even started yet, so I guess I'd better think seriously now as it is nearly 6 o'clock.

Trusting all is well with you and your family.

Love,

Dulcie

5th February 1970

Dear Fran,

What fun we had opening the parcel you sent. It arrived Christmas Eve while visitors were here. The space food was sampled by everyone and is delicious. Since school started, Terry's "Space

Pen" has been quite an item of interest. Thank you very much, Fran, and I trust you enjoyed unpacking yours as much as we did.

We are having rather a wet year. Just what the drought-stricken west wanted. Since New Year's Day we've had 43 inches [110 cm] of rain. We wanted the assistment [also agistment] cattle off the place and ordered the semi-trailers. What a time!

The big semis would not go the last ½ mile to the yards and we had to truck the cattle 10 at a time in the small truck and back onto the semis until they were loaded. Took us 3 days in rain and mud to load the 400. Anyway they are all gone and there's just our own stock to care for now.

Len went up to St. Lawrence last week to see my brother. Rain has poured down ever since and Len is unable to get home. The road report on the radio last night stated one bridge was 22 feet [6.7 metres] under water, and still rising 3 inches [7.5 cm] an hour, and it's still raining! Terry and I were going with him for the day but at the last minute I had a phone call to go to Rockhampton.

Aren't we glad now that we didn't go. One day turned into 2 weeks. Anyway he is okay and there's nothing he could do if he was home. I shifted the horses to higher ground yesterday and opened the gates on two extra paddocks for the cattle to get onto the hilly country and that is about all that can be done for a while.

Dad and I are going to cross the bridge in the tractor today to get food and mail over before it rises too high. Needless to say Terry is enjoying the fact that the school bus can't get over and so he has no school. The army helicopter still goes over every day so if there is any emergency we can always hang the flag up to bring him down. So we are not isolated really.

Do you remember me mentioning Terry's old collie dog at times, Fran? Poor old thing was 10 years old and for the past year she wasn't too well. She died 3 weeks ago very quietly in her sleep. We miss her about the place.

The working dogs, Queensland blue heelers, aren't to be petted and played with so we haven't any pet dog now. The old ginger cat who was about the same age died a few days ago too. The wet weather seemed to affect him and he had a cold.

Well, Fran, I have a few letters to get ready before Dad comes, so I must away.

Hope you are all well.

Love,

Dulcie

3rd April 1970

Dear Fran,

After waiting to hear from you about the parcel, I can only presume it didn't arrive. I'm so sorry Fran. I know if yours didn't reach us we would be unhappy. In our remote part of the world, your letters and Christmas parcel are eagerly looked forward to. It is a pity we are unable to insure our overseas parcels, as you can. I made inquiries at our local post office but of course they cannot trace the parcel. I went to Rockhampton yesterday and selected some more gifts for you. Unfortunately I couldn't get the same things as before and could only procure a small bear for you.

Nevertheless it is a bear and I'm set on the idea that you must have a bear! I hope this parcel will arrive in time for your birthday in August if not before. Please don't be too disappointed about the other one, Fran, just look forward to the next one.

We have had a very hectic time lately. I've been in hospital for 3 weeks with kidney trouble and Len was flat out coping with home and outside work. A disease has spread through the coastal cattle making them go down and unable to move for 5 or 6 days.

Going through the paddocks taking water and feed to them twice a day has kept us busy. So far we have 250 of them down. Dingos are troublesome at night, killing calves and biting and half-eating the sick ones. We laid out strychnine baits today but with the defenceless beasts about I don't think the dingos will eat the baits. The cruel devils would rather kill.

My two brothers and their families came to stay for the 4-day Easter break. I didn't get much time to talk to them unfortunately, having to leave home before they rose and getting back late at night.

Ann and Coral were wonderful though, always had the meal cooked when we came in at night and they finished my huge pile of ironing and other jobs I just couldn't catch up on after being away in hospital.

Well, Fran, I must hurry as Len is ready to go again after this lunch break.

I hope this parcel will not disappear.

Love,

Dulcie

23rd April 1970

Dear Fran,

Many thanks for your letter and the greeting card.

I agree with you, we are getting old. I'm like an old car, pieces wearing out inside and the bodywork all dents and scratches. Still, guess we will hang together for a few more years.

Hope your diet is working well for you, Fran. My mother often goes on a diet but never sticks to it long enough to do any good. Still it is worse to be like me, 5 feet 6 inches [168 cm] tall and weighing 112 pounds [51 kg]. Len calls me "Old Skinny". Oh well, when I retire and have nothing to do - maybe I'll get to be "Old Fatty"!

I can imagine Ricky being excited about his bike. Terry loves motors too and he has been driving the car and truck for over a year now. One advantage in having a property, he is able to drive miles anywhere on it but not on the road until he turns 17. Then he can get a drivers' licence.

He still plays the recorder and guitar and plays football, cricket and swims for the Yeppoon Primary team. He was elected Captain of the Primary Science team as well. He started school with the idea of becoming a scientist and he is still bearing that way.

Has been raining here for over a week now and everything is

damp and mouldy. Just one day of sunshine would be nice. Well, Fran, it's out into the rain to work again.

So love till next time,
Dulcie

16th September 1970

Dear Fran,

Wonderful to hear from you again and to read all about your travels during the holidays. The snaps are so nice too.

Summer is well and truly with us again, with century temps [38°C] and only a few dry thunderstorms so far. Bad seasons and stock losses have forced Len to go away to work again. He is working for the Broads and Shire Council near Mackay - quite an easy job - truck driving. He likes it very much. Drives home Friday nights and goes back Sunday afternoons. So we do see him each weekend.

Makes the work here seem doubly hard after having him home for over a year. Bush fires were bad about a month ago and Terry and I worked day and night for three days, on tractor and dozer, making fire breaks to head it off. But all to no avail as it finally burnt right through our property.

Fortunately with the new bores we put down last year, the stock have plenty of water but I'm kept busy carting hay and fodder out each day. Stock losses have been heavy, especially cows with calves. Makes it hard as I have to shoot the calf when its mother dies.

Dingos are not troubling us too badly as I've kept the baits laid out. They killed my pet calf in the house paddock last week. He was just a calf, I know, but I was fond of him and cried when I had to burn his little body.

Len sent a message via the radio telephone on Tuesday. His Holden had broken a timing cog in the motor, 192 miles [309 km] from here, when he was on his way back to work last Sunday. He had it towed into a cattle property "Garmount" and asked if I could go up and tow it home.

I obtained a permit from the police for Terry to steer it while I towed and we went up yesterday and brought it home. It was a long, tiring, hot day and Terry was utterly exhausted when we reached home last night. The road is extremely bad, rough and stony with deep pot holes, and it took us 5 and ½ hours to get there after leaving home at 4:30 a.m. Took us 2 hours to set up the tow and have lunch and 9 hours to make the journey home by 8:30 pm.

The slowest part was the pull over the Great Dividing Range - over 20 miles [32 km] in the lowest gear with the engine boiling all the way. However we had no serious trouble and Terry did a mighty job for an 11 year old. He had a bath while I made his tea and then went to bed while I carted hay to the stock until 3 am then started the water pumps.

Wasn't worth going to bed then so I let Terry sleep in and miss another day's school and started in on the usual work today. Had a few minutes sleep in between jobs today but am looking forward to bed tonight.

Meanwhile Len's car is safely at home and he will get a ride down to Rockhampton Friday night with a friend so I can pick him up and have the parts ready to fix his car over the weekend.

Just wasn't our lucky day - one of the engines on the water pump broke down last night, too. Was nearly daylight before I got it going. Had broken the key out of the keyway that holds the flywheel on.

Fortunately, we had a spare one so I had it going about 4 am while all the stock in that paddock waited and kept me company, looking for water. Poor things, they are so trusting, just seemed to know that I was fixing it and waited patiently for a drink.

Well, Fran, think I'll go to bed. Do write. I love to hear from you even though I don't get around to writing very often.

Love,
Dulcie

———✗——✗——✗——

11th November 1970

Dear Fran,

It's so hot today and being busy makes the heat seem worse. During the lunch hour I came back to the house to try and catch up with a few house jobs. Started the generating engine and finished the ironing and I am now waiting for meat pie and cakes to finish baking. With the big diesel engine thumping, and the heat, I have quite a headache.

Something I've always meant to ask you, Fran. Do parts of US lack electricity the same as most country areas here? Or is it because our farms, etc. are so big with so few people living on them that it is not profitable for the electricity authorities to take the power into the country? We nearly all have private power plants run by engines to generate electricity.

Most people have the low voltage ones, 32V, but in the last 3 or 4 years the 240V ones have become very popular. All town areas are 240V and so the radios, TV, washing machines, refrigerators, etc. are all made for this. Anyone with a 32V plant must pay extra to have these things altered to run on low voltage.

I really don't envy you your job as tax consultant, Fran! Makes me shudder to think of the time I have when I must file our tax at the end of June each year. Horrible! Horrible! Depreciation on this, that and everything else. Income derived from sale of cattle, fodder and other produce, loss from crop failure and stock deaths. Income from other sources, deductions for everything. Brainwave! I may send it all over to you! Anyway, Fran, good luck with it. I sincerely hope you find it profitable and interesting.

We have an election day next Saturday, too. Senate elections. There's been talk of lowering the voting age to 18 here, too. Not only the voting age but adult age to 18 instead of 21 as it is now. I really can't see any harm in a lower voting age, but I most certainly do not agree that anyone of 18 should be classed as an adult and allowed to handle financial affairs, etc.

No, we don't seem to have much time for musical entertainment anymore. Since Tom married and had to settle down to steady work, we haven't seen very much of him. Coral (his wife) often drives out to see us but usually I'm away working and just find a note she has left.

Len came home for a weekend 2 weeks ago. Brought a baby parrot he'd found fallen from its nest and a horrible big lizard with spikes and lumps all over it. I named it Len Lizard and it lives in the rockery. The little parrot is growing feathers now and goes everywhere with me (so I can feed the little pest). He or she is such a happy little thing and sings most of the day.

Terry has guinea pigs, a possum, a bandicoot and a wallaby (plus pigeons and white mice, caged) all running about the garden, too. I often think that one of these days there will be a big fight between the lot. Old Sugarplum, the house cat, seems to tolerate them all, although he sometimes looks longingly into the glass mouse-house!

Terry is doing his final exams for the year this week and school breaks up for 7 weeks holiday on December 11th. He is looking forward to the break as this year has been most tiring for him also. The long dry season and the heat are bad enough but he has been extra busy helping me.

When he gets home at 5 pm he takes the Land Rover down to start the water engines on each water point. It is quite dark by the time I've turned the horse loose and he picks me up to come home. We got him an electronic project kit a few weeks ago and he loves to tinker with it and make things but there's so little time. So the vacation will be good for him.

I have some of my Christmas shopping done already and I must get your parcel away before the end of the month. I hope it fares better than last year's did!

Well, Fran, my baking is done and I have 300 head of cattle to push through the dip before dark (curse the fellow who brought ticks to Australia!) with the hinderance of a dead finger. Beating a cold chisel though a piece of steel yesterday and missed. Took the side off my finger and I had to go into Yeppoon and get 2 stitches in it. Can't say it is very sore but am trying to keep it clean and dry as the Doc advised. Quite an effort for me!

Hope you are all doing well, Fran and do write soon.

Love,

Dulcie

PS Our transport service has been cancelled and we have to go to Yeppoon for our mail now. So we have a box number and a very simple address now.

3rd February 1971

Dear Fran,

What excitement your parcel caused! Our creek, two miles from the house, has been well over the bridge for days and we haven't been able to get to Yeppoon. One day the post office phoned regarding a registered parcel they were holding and would we please claim it. When we found out it was from the USA, Terry and I hopped into the truck and walked over the flooded bridge to leave Terry safe. Then I removed the fan belt and covered the distributor and drove the truck through.

We collected the parcel, stocked up with supplies and headed for home in pouring rain. However the creek had risen much too high so we camped the night in the truck. Wet and cold and bitten by thousands of mosquitoes but we were quite happy as we had your parcel to open and were thrilled with everything in it.

We used the little collapsible cup to mix up the orange drink "Start" and the little pocket knife to slice up the food we'd bought. Then we read the Journal and Cook Book and Terry ate sweets and chewed gum till he went to sleep propped up in the corner. Thank you so much for everything, Fran.

At daylight I walked over (or should say half-swam over) the bridge to home and returned with the tractor and towed Terry home in the truck. This was on January 27th and we haven't been able to cross since so Terry has had time off from school. We've had 2152 points of rain [20.5 inches or 52 cm] since January 20th and it's still coming down hard.

Len went back to work on January 16th, out near Blackwater somewhere. They sent him and I haven't heard from him but phoned the firm and was told all the truck drivers are isolated but quite okay. Anyway this should see an end to the crippling drought in that area at least.

Drying clothes is a bit of a problem. Most things we don't need urgently I've left to hang out but other items of clothing are hanging in the sheds along with Terry's pets. Mice, possum, bandicoot, turtle, lizard, cats and birds had to all go into the shed together (in separate cages of course).

I fastened a guide chain along one side of the bridge the other day so now I can phone someone to meet me with mail and food, etc. and walk over to get it in safety. Was a little dangerous before with nothing to hold onto and the water has quite a current.

So Fran, I'd better close and get the other mail ready to take over tomorrow. Strangely enough, Fran, even with all this rain I don't envy you your winter! Shudder! 40 degrees [4°C] and warm! you said. Gosh, how do you survive?

Write soon and love from,

Dulcie

6th May 1971

Dear Fran,

Was so nice to hear from you again. I love to read about your trips. The roads must be wonderful over there and it seems you can drive hundreds of miles in a few hours. Here it is a tiring journey to drive over 35 miles [56 km]. I wonder if Australia will ever have completely sealed roads? Even our main and only highway, No 1, is only sealed in some sections and not wide enough for two cars to pass, unless one gets onto the gravel edge. Overseas visitors have named it the Crystal Highway because it is strewn with broken windscreen glass.

Thank you, too, for the lovely card, Fran. I really had a good birthday. Being a Wednesday I had steers to truck to the Gracemere Sales Yard.

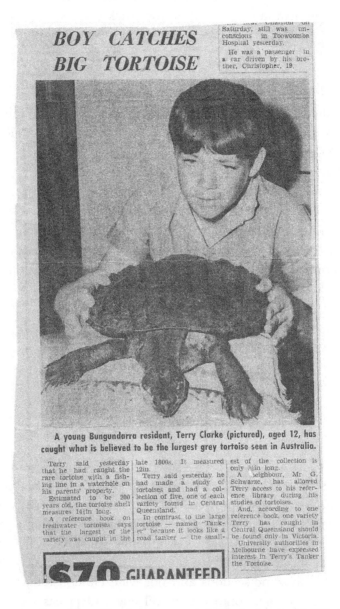

BOY CATCHES BIG TORTOISE

Saturday, still was un-conscious in Toowoomba Hospital yesterday.

He was a passenger in a car driven by his bro-ther, Christopher, 19.

A young Bungundarra resident, Terry Clarke (pictured), aged 12, has caught what is believed to be the largest grey tortoise seen in Australia.

Terry said yesterday that he had caught the rare tortoise with a fish-ing line in a waterhole on his parents' property.

Estimated to be 200 years old, the tortoise shell measures 14¼in long.

A reference book on freshwater tortoises says that the largest of the variety was caught in the late 1800s. It measured 12in.

Terry said yesterday he had made a study of tortoises and had a col-lection of five, one of each variety found in Central Queensland.

In contrast to the large tortoise — named "Tank-er" because it looks like a road tanker — the small-est of the collection is only 4½in long.

A neighbour, Mr G. Schwarze, has allowed Terry access to his refer-ence library during his studies of tortoises.

And, according to one reference book, one variety Terry has caught in Central Queensland should be found only in Victoria.

University authorities in Melbourne have expressed interest in Terry's Tanker the Tortoise.

$70 GUARANTEED

Terry took a day off school to watch his being sold. We had to get out of bed at 3 am, drive down to the yards, and load the steers.

Then drive the 45 miles [72 km] to Gracemere and unload and then back for another load as our truck can only carry 14 big ones.

Anyway we got dressed up with the last load and reached the yard in time for the start of the sale at 10:30. Was rather hectic and we hadn't had any breakfast. Our steers were sold at 1 pm. Terry got $130 each for his 4 and Len's 24 brought $144 each. So it wasn't too bad.

While talking to our stock agent, Terry remarked that it was my birthday so the agent took Terry and I to lunch at an Oriental Restaurant. Was a lovely meal and I felt happy but tired driving the big rough truck home that afternoon.

More surprises to come, however, when we got home just on sunset. Coral and Tom arrived to take Terry and I to a surprise birthday dinner. Oh heck, after the day's work and the oriental lunch! Anyway by 8 pm we had all the work done and out we went again. Had a lovely time and fell into bed at 1:30 am. Gosh, what a long day. Still I think it's about the nicest birthday I've had.

Just as well Len had forgotten it, as usual, otherwise we may have had another night out when he came home that weekend. As it was we had a day out on the Sunday.

We went fishing and I caught 14 bream, about 4-pound [2 kg] ones, and Len caught 19. Terry was unlucky, he only got 7 but he also got 2 lovely big crabs. I like crab better than fish, especially small fish like these.

Still is was a nice day and we enjoyed the little fish for a couple of days' dinners. Better luck next time I hope! The oysters were all dead too, so disappointing. The heavy run off of fresh water into the sea kills the delicious creatures.

Well, Fran, the moths and bugs are bad tonight and Sugarplum is chasing them all over my desk so I guess I'll wrap up this letter before he completely destroys it.

Lots of love from,
Dulcie

20th August 1971

Dear Fran,

It's so long since I've heard from you. I do hope everything is alright. Perhaps as it is summer over there, you are just enjoying yourselves.

Winter hasn't been too bad this year. We had only 2 or 3 frosty mornings and have had quite a bit of rain, including a thunderstorm, so apparently winter has passed us by. Thank heavens!

Terry goes back to school on 23rd after his winter 2-week break. He went for 1 week with his father to Blackwater, where Len is working at present, and this week Terry is spending at home.

Len's mother has been with me for a few weeks to help me.

I burnt both hands with boiling tar some weeks ago and I can describe it with one word, Painful (with a capital P).

The right hand is coming along quite well now, although only the thumb and first 2 fingers are out of bandages. The left one is still painful but shows no sign of getting well enough to "patch" yet.

I'm so useless without hands and it's making me angry just sitting about. My dad's hand has healed completely now. Only took his 12 weeks to heal at his age so I think mine should too!

Before this happened - the Yeppoon show was on in May and we entered a few things to help make a show.

The old cat Sugarplum won a 2nd prize (in just the common pet cat section).

My Braford bull, Chewys, won his section in the pure-bred class and Len came 2nd in the wood-chop. He was handicapped by 15 seconds.

Well, Fran, Happy Birthday and do write soon.

Love,

Dulcie

PS Thought you might like the cuttings from the paper. Len is where I have put an X.

The chips were flying in this tree felling contest at the Yeppoon Show yesterday.

—✳——✳——✳—

1st February 1972

Dear Fran,

Well, the holidays are over once again and so far this new year has been a very busy one. Christmas was rather nice this year. It was fairly cool and rainy weather and my parents, Len's parents and a young German friend (who comes every year for Christmas) had quite a lovely day. After dinner the parents and Len had a nap and John (our friend), Terry and I played Monopoly.

Boxing Day was not so good as we had the first warning of a cyclone off the coast. For two days we had terrific wind and rain then the cyclone moved north to Townsville and really wrecked the town, killing 4 people. When the wind eased here we spent days mending fences and cutting off fallen trees, getting bogged, dipping cattle, etc. Then we dismantled the Holden and put a new engine in it. Planted Pangola-grass in the rain for a few days. It doesn't grow by seed and must be planted by cuttings. It is doing well now.

Len went back to work, driving 252 miles [405 km] on 20th January, and was held up by flooded bridges for two days. He had plenty of food with him so he was ok. Terry started at the Secondary school on 24th and so far he likes it. He is very lucky with his foreign language subject, German, as I can read, write and speak it too. And if I'm not available to help in the afternoons, young John is always here after work to watch TV so Terry gets help from him.

I spent all yesterday and this morning trying to get an engine going for John - no luck - I must admit this one defeats me. We haven't any like this one, a Japanese brand, Honda, and after seeing a Japanese engine, I sure wouldn't buy one! Looks like he will have to take it to a garage although he says he can't afford to. I suppose he finds things a bit hard now. He only left Germany 5 years ago and three and a half years ago bought 40 acres [16 hectares] about 5 miles [8 km] to the east of us. Must be hard to leave one's country and start afresh in a strange land with strange customs.

Must be the time for all engines to voice their complaints as our diesel lighting motor cut out a few nights ago which meant we had no electricity, no lights, no TV, etc. Had to give it a valve grind and new injector kit and it's going again. Strange how Australia uses 240 volt power, even our home plants. We can be electrocuted by it yet most of Europe and even your country manages with 110V to 120V. Wonder why?

We were thrilled with your parcel, Fran. The beer is much lighter than ours and quite palatable. You always manage to send things to delight us but we can't seem to find anything unusual to send you. Thank you so very much for everything, Fran.

Now I must away and get the tea dishes washed as Terry and John have finished with TV and it will soon be time for bed.

Lots of love,
Dulcie

10th March 1972

Dear Fran,

Autumn is here and the days are getting cooler. The nights are quite cold already and I've had to dig out the blankets. Seems we may have an early winter.

The year hasn't been too good for Terry so far. He came home 3 days ago after spending 4 weeks in hospital with rheumatic fever. Another week at home and he will be allowed to return to school but no sports or running about. His studies have of course fallen behind and it remains to be seen if he can catch up or slip a grade. However as long as his health is okay studies can come later.

I missed him and for the first time in my life I felt lonely when he was away. I even caught myself talking to Sugarplum! Now I know how lots of elderly folk feel when they live alone, specially the nights. Still, while visiting him and being alone at night I was able to get my winter woollies knitted. Pullovers for Terry and Len, in their chosen colours of green, and one for me. Also some baby knits for Tom's wife Coral who is expecting the infant in July.

You were quite right - the candied substance in the package was ginger. We grow it and some I candy or preserve in syrup. Last year's crop wasn't so good as the horses broke into the garden and ate the tops from the ginger which of course sets the root system back and the roots are what we eat.

Please be careful about taking an extra job, Fran. Believe me, when you know how much work this entails. By the time one has finished outside and still has the home to run, sometimes there's only three or four hour's sleep to be had and until you adjust to this it can be very rough. I wish you all the best though. Now I must hurry as I have work to do.

So lots of love,
Dulcie

5th May 1972

Dear Fran,

Lovely to hear from you again and many thanks for the card and birthday wishes. Gosh! your boys are really young men, Fran. Makes me feel quite aged to think it's only a few years since their pictures showed them as toddlers. When you think about it I have reached the half-way mark in life. Unfortunately I've too many things to do before I can retire to my rocking chair.

We've had over a week of terribly windy days. Great gusts make the house shudder and blows the fruit from the trees and breaks my flowers. One needs to be watchful when out working in the timbered country. Quite a few limbs falling.

Australia has Federal elections coming up on May 27th. I think we can do with a change of government so I hope my vote removes Mr. McMahon from office.

Terry has 2 weeks of winter holidays so he went back to work with Len last week. He is fascinated with Len's new truck. A great ugly 10-ton [10,160 kg] Toyota Tipper diesel. When Len has it at home occasionally, Terry drives it around helping his Dad repair our roads. We have roads all around the boundary fences and internal ones criss-cross all over the place to water troughs, etc.

Terry can't have a driver's licence to drive on proper roads, of course, but anyone can drive any kind of vehicle - registered or not - on their own property. Terry has his own "bomb" to burn around the place in, an ancient 1957 Holden. The old thing runs well but he never keeps a muffler on it and I can hear him coming a mile off!

Len's favourite "bomb" is the old Zephyr also without a muffler and when the two of them take off, so do my ears.

Well, Fran, as I have the whole place to myself, guess I'll start the generator, get a bite to eat and watch whatever I want to on TV for once, before bedtime.

Write soon.

Lots of love,

Dulcie

25th October 1972

Dear Fran,

It's months since you wrote about your illness and operation. Many times I've meant to write you, but there just never seems to be time.

Every day I think of you and wonder just how you are. Strange how we have never met, and probably never will, but I always think of you as my closest friend. Perhaps it's because I don't see many people. Sometimes I don't see another person, apart from Terry, for months.

How do you feel now, anyway? My mum had the same operation years ago, but she recovered and has no discomfort in the area at all. Still you have the children to care for, so more work than she had. Try to take things easy, Fran.

I'm still hale and hearty as ever. Just growing old and getting tired.

The heat and dry weather have us almost ready to give in. With an annual rainfall of 65 inches [170 cm], we've only had 16 inches [41 cm] so far, and this country can't live without its rainfall.

I've been hand-feeding the cattle for months and got through winter with very few losses. With an average of 2 hours rest at night, and 2 hours daily, I can handle the feeding, water, irrigation of fodder and harvesting.

For how long I don't know as the water position is drastic now.

The ninety-six foot [29 metres] deep bore for the house supply is completely dry. Two bores for stock water are dry and only 2 dams have water still. Only one bore has water now and I'm irrigating fodder but its almost useless for that now and completely out of the question for drinking, either stock or humans. The salt content is now killing the crops.

For the house I have to use the truck with a 1500-gallon [5678 litres] tank fitted to cart water from Yeppoon. The town council charge ½ cent per gallon [4 litres] but the long haul home over that road makes it a slow trip. The truck's engine is not in the best order and it finds it hard going. I only hope the old thing doesn't bail up altogether. The little 4-ton [4064 kg] truck can't handle the job if the big one goes.

So I just hope for rain.

The biggest bush fire I've seen for 14 years went through most of this area a few weeks ago. How it started is anyone's guess. I spent days on the dozer putting in fire breaks, when the fire was still miles away. Terry drove the dozer for hours at night too. Put up a really good effort.

But with a strong wind for days, the fire travelled at a terrific pace, burning night and day. Our fire breaks were useless. The flames just leaped across one after another.

It reached our boundary at 11 am on a day with a temp of 105°F [41°C] and a humidity reading of 6. Almost suffocated us. When the flames came into our property, we knew our stock would be killed. With the grass all tinder-dry and thick, they would roast. Smoke made the horses panic and I was able to catch only one mare bred here and used to fire.

Terry stayed at the house and called the fire brigade and neighbours. The mare took me through the smoke and we picked up mobs of cattle wherever they were hanging on fences. I drove them at a gallop to the area with shorter grass where the flames were not so high. They went through the flames to safety where the fire had already burnt.

The flames were leaping up trees, burning from top to top and I couldn't get into some paddocks. I could only take the wire cutters from the saddle bag and cut the barbs wherever possible and hope the cattle could run for their lives - anywhere.

Looking back, even the terrible times had some funny moments. Like when I circled back to the cattle yard and barns. The firemen, neighbours and my parents were there. They had saved the buildings.

My mother had been crying and was quite sure she would never see me alive. But when I rode in all she could say was, "Oh, she saved Bluey and a calf."

Bluey, the cattle dog, always hitches a ride in front of the saddle after a day's work. And somewhere along the way that day I had picked up a new born calf and had it on the front with Bluey sitting on top of it. Guess it did look strange!

Anyway all the buildings were saved, and the machinery. But so far I've found a good many stock, especially calves and foals, burned to death. Still a lot missing. But as the fire continued to burn right through to the coast - everyone cut their fences - so it will take a long time to round them all up and sort them out.

As water is scarce everywhere, it's easy to find them at my water hole or trough. Now there is no grass for them so I'm feeding them molasses. Most of the neighbours are selling their stock to the meat works as they round them up. But I'll be hanged if I'll sell the ones I've selected and bred for eight years. They are stud stock and no meat works will get them.

We are more fortunate than others, as Len is still away working, so we are not without some money to keep going. Two other neighbours are doing the same. The rest have to sell because their wives and families can't handle the work alone.

Len came home to see how we were doing last weekend. I haven't seen him since July. He looks quite well considering he has to cook his own meals. Ugh! What a cook!

Well, Fran, I've been writing this letter sitting on top of the water truck waiting for it to fill. It's now 1:30 in the morning, the town is quiet and there's a lovely sea breeze. However, I'll have to leave it now and head for home.

Terry is asleep at home. Len's mother is staying with us for a while which is really good as she sees that we have meals.

Looking at the calendar in the truck, I just realised Brendan would have been 10 years old today.

Fran, do take care of yourself and remember even when I don't write to you, that I still think of you every day.

Lots of love from,

Dulcie

18th December 1972

Dear Fran,

Sorry, I didn't realise that Christmas was so near. The days and nights just pass and only for Len's mum reminding me to do this and that on certain days, none of the office work would get done or any mail sent.

It's much cooler tonight or perhaps I should say today since it is 2:10 am according to the truck's clock. Only 70 degrees [21°C] now. Was 105 [41°C] in the truck today and it boiled the radiator dry all day. I'm pumping out the load of water for the cattle.

Wish you could see the kangaroos, emus and wallabies and other things all drinking with the cattle, Fran. They are so hungry and thirsty. They eat molasses with the stock too and are so quiet. They don't eat or drink all that much so I don't kill them.

My favourites are the little kanga-rats. They are so friendly and will eat from my hand and hop into the car when Terry comes with lucerne.

Sorry about the spelling, Fran, I'm too tired to think straight and anyway the torch light is poor.

Anyhow, I just wanted to wish you all a Merry Christmas and Happy New Year. Hope the New Year brings inches of rain too.

Mum packed a parcel for you and I mailed it - can't remember just when but a few weeks ago, I think.

I hope it reaches you in time for Christmas, Fran.

Have a nice time and best wishes.
Love,
Dulcie

—※——※——※—

15th February 1973

Dear Fran,

What a lovely start to the day, we got your parcel! All the goodies to eat and the Eve cigarettes are so beautiful. I've never seen cigarettes with flowers before. Terry loved his car-kit and begged the candy jar for his bottle collection. We had a lovely time unpacking and admiring everything. Thank you so much, Fran.

Can't see too good tonight, Fran, so please excuse the writing. While using the electric welder today I caught a flash in the eyes. The right eye in particular is nearly driving me mad.

This afternoon just wasn't my day. All the vehicles and machinery decided to break down. Even my car. Cursed Valiant, never did like the thing. Backed out of the shed today to go to Yeppoon and blew the left front brake hose. Plugged it off and drove in anyway. Fixed that after lunch, then the turning lights [indicators] wouldn't work. After that the starter motor packed in and to cap it off the clutch plate busted. Pushed it in the shed and left it. Hope the thing dissolves into thin air overnight.

We had 16 inches [41 cm] of rain since 14th of January. The grass is so beautiful. Never thought I'd see green grass again. Still it hurts to think of all the animals who are not alive to enjoy it.

It's amazing and wonderful to know that people do care though. After the fire and the press coverage that followed, Old Henrietta (the goat) who lost her baby kid in the fire, attracted the attention of so many wonderful townsfolk. They would come to meet me, even during the night while filling the water truck, with left over bread and bundles of grass and even vegetables to give her. With the few teeth she has left, she devoured it all and kept in good condition. Now I have many new friends who often call to see Henrietta. And the old dear enjoys all of her visitors. I'll mate her again soon and hope she enjoys life long enough to see her baby grow up.

The world's money problems are in quite a state at the moment. What with the Australian dollar rising 7 per cent and the US dollar falling 10 per cent it is difficult to say what will eventuate. It means we will get less for the beef we sell to the USA but I guess you won't be able to buy it any cheaper in the meat shops there. Always hits the consumers' pockets hard.

Well, Fran, guess it's not much use worrying about these things. Anyway, my eye is enough to worry about for now. My weakest part must be my eyes. Can stand most things but this is TOO MUCH. Will go through the medicine cabinet and try everything, one after another. Might help.

Thank you for your letter and the parcel, Fran.

Love,

Dulcie

10th April 1973

Dear Fran,

Your letter mentioning food prices was most interesting. We, too, have the problem of making the money go around. I've enclosed some cuttings for you.

Considering our national wage is $57 - $85 per week, you can see the troubles wage earners have. Primary producers, such as we, can buy petrol and diesel in bulk. But not less than 44 gallons [166 litres] a time at wholesale rates which is 10 cents per gallon [4 litres] cheaper than wage-earning average citizens. Our meat is perhaps not quite as expensive as over there but still out of range for those on low income.

Pensioners (old age) here receive a fortnightly cheque for $37.50 for a married couple. This gives them only $18.50 per week to live on. Those paying rent on a room consisting of 1 bedroom, small kitchen, bath and toilet facilities (mostly $8 to $10) are entitled to another $4 per week. No wonder half of them starve to death. Terry's school text books this year totalled $103. School fees $53-$75 and the first term is not over yet with 2 more to go. His school uniform shirts are $5.75 each, shorts $6.50, shoes $13.95, plus socks, hat, etc. MY! How are we going to survive this way?

Well, Fran, I must away as I have killed a pig and it should be ready to cut up for the freezer now.

Love,
Dulcie

29th August 1973

Dear Fran,

I did send you a card for your birthday but at that time there were no spare minutes to write. So if this reached you in time, again, let me wish you a happy birthday and many more.

I just received your letter and I'm so sorry that thieves robbed you. I've always said that I could forgive most of the sinners against society, sometimes even a murderer, but never a thief. To me a person who steals is the lowest type. When one spends a lifetime working hard to accumulate possessions and then some loafing drop-out comes along and takes them, believe me I'd shoot to kill anyone who tried to steal our things.

Yes, Fran, cars and all machinery are expensive to run and repair. The only reason I've learned to repair machinery is because it saves money. Len has never been a good mechanic. He doesn't have the patience to repair anything and breaks more than he sets out to fix. But Dad was good and he taught my two brothers and myself, when we were children, that to repair breakages at home was cheaper and more convenient than going to a garage or service station.

The boys were taught to cook, sew, knit, embroider, etc. just as I was taught to do boy's work. How we have blessed our parents for this! Terry too, has been taught to shoot, drive, service and repair machinery and all the other things a boy should do as well as cook a 3-course meal, sew, wash and iron clothes and all the other household chores.

In later years he may be grateful, although at present he hates what he calls "Women's Work".

Yes, Fran, Terry is growing up fast. He is far taller and heavier than I, more like his father's build. He is 5 feet 10 inches [180 cm] tall and weighs 10 stone (or 140 pounds) [63.5 kg] against Len's 6 feet 1 inch [185 cm], 196 pounds [89 kg] and my 5 feet 6 inches [168 cm], 119 pounds [54 kg]. He is a good help to me, doing well at school with his Technical A course, but so far has no set plans for the future.

He often has one or two boys from town (school mates) out to stay for the weekend. One can't help but notice the difference though. The lads from town have never had the chance to learn to shoot, drive, fish, ride horses, etc. and Terry has had to make them take turns for weekend visits, as all of the boys would like to come at once.

Terry spent 2 weekends in town on return visits but won't go again, as he said he was hungry all weekend. I guess we country folk are lucky that we produce most of our food and we have plenty of it.

Still the townsfolk have more luxuries than us. New furniture for the home every so often and holidays each year. We haven't had a holiday since we went fruit picking when Brendan died in March 1963. With petrol (or I think you call it gas) at 61 cents a gallon, oil at $2.76 a gallon and tyres at $30 each we spend that money growing things to eat instead of holidaying.

Food prices are alarming here as apparently they are over there. Funny thing though, Fran, the farmer isn't getting any more than he did 10 years ago. It's the middle man who is getting the profit.

When we sell cattle, we still get the same price as we always did, but the butcher sells it to the housewives for double what he paid for it. The government cries "inflation" all the time yet no one inquires into it, to see who is getting the benefit.

Makes me wonder whether all the politicians own shops!

Well, Fran, enough raving about the government. One party is as bad as the other anyway.

Hope you are all well and again many happy returns.

Love,

Dulcie

28th September 1973

Dear Fran,

It is 9:30 pm and here I sit, in the car, in front of the Yeppoon Town Hall, waiting for Terry. The High School students have a social evening every so often and Terry loves to come in for the dancing, etc. Makes a long day but the young ones must have some fun.

Strangely enough I seem to be the only one waiting here. Since adults are not invited to the social, all the parents have gone to the hotel to fill in time. Since I have to drive, I'll wait till I get home for a cold beer.

Electricity seems to have gone mad everywhere this week. Our own light system isn't going too good due to water in the diesel line. The alternator on the car is playing up so I hesitate to use the interior light to write and now the town power seems to have a weakness. The street light is so dull I can hardly see and then next thing it comes on real brilliant!

We didn't have much in the way of winter - thank heavens - but summer is sure coming on strong. With only the first month of spring gone the temp has been mostly in the late 80's [27°C] and the last week every day over 90 degrees [32°C]. Still we have had good rain and very little frost so grass is plentiful.

I wish you could see all the little white Brahman calves, Fran, they are so beautiful with their big ears hanging down and they are so friendly and trusting. They love to be petted. One born today makes a total of 120 calves so far this spring. I'm glad I kept their mothers during the drought even though it was hard work. The little goats too are growing like mushrooms and are so beautiful.

I almost forgot again, Fran, last time I wrote, Terry asked me to ask if Ricky, Mark, or Dick could assist him with his bullet collection. He collects all calibre bullets and shells, fired or not, from pistols, rifles or machine guns and cannon and if Dick and the boys want to exchange he has some spares. One of the hardest bullets to get here is a .44 rifle bullet which we are told is commonly used in USA.

Well, Fran, the children are starting to come out now, so I guess I'd better close and drop this into the post office on the way home.

Lots of love,
Dulcie

PART IV

1974 - 1981

25th April 1974

Dear Fran

Thank you so much for the birthday wishes. I'm so sorry you did not receive my letter posted during the February floods. Guess it was just one of the many things that disappeared at that time. We enjoyed everything in your parcel, including the note paper, some of which I am returning to you.

Today is Anzac Day in Australia - a public holiday. Services are held at all churches and servicemen and women and school children march through the towns and cities to the cenotaphs where wreaths are laid and the last-post is played to honour the dead from New Zealand and Australia in all wars.

It is good to know your children are growing up too! Makes me feel that I am not alone in the world facing this problem. Terry is in 3rd year of High School and does reasonably well in his studies. He takes English, Advanced Maths, Technical Drawing, Science A and Science B, Citizenship Education and Metal Work. He is captain of the softball team and the cricket team and plays number 2 (right winger) in rugby league football.

He is not difficult - apart from playing his cassette and radio too loud. As a matter of fact I really don't know how all the work would be done if it wasn't for Terry. Being an only child he is so precious. I guess they are no matter if one has a dozen and it's hard to realise he is grown up and wants freedom.

Last Christmas he bought himself a new rifle and wanted to go shooting alone. It took me some time to allow it and even now I find myself listening for sounds of his car (which has no exhaust system) and if he is a minute overdue, I worry like mad. Still, he is a reliable and careful boy but accidents do happen.

Strangely enough, he has a soft spot for all the baby things and when he shoots anything (pests only), no matter how big a pest or a thing is, he always brings the babies home. After we have reared them we have a waiting list of zoos which will take them, thank heavens! Still, we become attached to them and I have kept some. All told, 10 animals - bandicoots, wallabies and kangaroos are running around our garden, steadily destroying the lawn. Guess I'll have to do something about locking them up in a paddock of their own.

One kangaroo we have had since he was a tiny thing with no hair and will insist on hopping inside the house, dragging his dirty muddy tail! When I scold him, he puts out his paws and hugs me. Spoilt thing!

Well, Fran, I must go to bed and many thanks again for remembering my birthday and for the Christmas parcel.

Take care and love from,

Dulcie

19th July 1974

Dear Fran,

So nice to hear from you again. Guess I've been a bit down in the dumps this last week. We all had influenza. It took about 2 weeks to pass off and then I had to get a relapse and ended up in hospital with pneumonia for 13 days. Wasn't alone there anyway. My brother, Tom, landed in with the same thing two days after me. Unbelievable! The toughest two in the family.

For a few days I didn't care very much but afterwards I wondered how my animals were getting along. They are not used to being fed by anyone else, not even Terry. Len did his best with everything. The only real trouble he had was with two little kangaroos that are still being bottle fed. Len said the little devils hated him and wouldn't eat until Terry got home from school.

He somehow didn't get around to searching for my puppy, Augy, every day and one morning found him paralyzed in the back and legs from tick bites. He took him to the only vet available in Yeppoon at the moment, Dr. Cordell. He recently came from Texas (USA). He gave Augy anti-tick toxin injections and kept him for 3 days then phoned Len and said he thought it best to destroy him.

Len thought the little fellow had a chance and brought him home. He said as soon as Augy saw his mates (a kangaroo and Sugarplum) he brightened up and began to eat, although it took days before his legs would work again. The American Vet admitted he had not had experience with ticks before. Anyway Augy is well now. Funny little ugly cross-breed, he is good for nothing really, but we all love him.

The Iwasaki Tourist Scheme has been blocked by the Federal Government pending a full inquiry into what useful purpose it would serve. Yes, Fran we are with our neighbour, John Dalton, in the Yeppoon Protection Council and we wholeheartedly object to this development of the Japanese.

The State Government seems to have been bought over by the Japanese and are willing to sell every acre of Queensland land to overseas interests. This I can't agree with, whether they be Japanese, British, American or any other overseas interest. Should the individual foreigner wish to purchase land to reside on then okay. But for a large area to be held by foreigners while living in their own countries, then I object.

We have many people from all nations living in and about Yeppoon. For instance the vet is American, so are 3 farmers, 4 neighbours are German and friends further on are Italian, Czechs, Poles but these people live and work on the land they bought and good luck to them.

We believe the Japanese do not intend to use all this land for a tourist resort (16,000 acres [6475 hectares] how could they!) but just to hold the land for future use. After all, in 50 years time, land will be valuable.

Up to this time the Federal Government blocked the scheme. The Japanese were still offering ridiculous prices for land. One and a $\frac{1}{4}$ million dollars for John Dalton's and 1 and $\frac{1}{2}$ million for ours. I could just see my grandchildren down on their knees begging for a piece of land to build on and no way would we sell to an overseas interest.

Well, Fran, guess I must feed my animals since they are all showing me how much they love me now I'm home. Make them appreciate me, the devils! Write soon.

Love,
Dulcie

———✗————✗————✗———

1 November 1974

Dear Fran,

How are you all? I can't quite remember who owes who a letter but I have time to write while sitting with Terry. Winter is over at last, (thank heaven!) although summer hasn't really got off to a good start health-wise. Our virus flu dragged on for months and after I came out of hospital I still had it for weeks. I almost coughed the roof off the house.

Now, to start summer, Terry is ill and the school called (phoned I should say) Mum last Monday to say that Terry had taken ill and was admitted to hospital. When I came home from work Mum had been and left a note. Strange how one imagines the worst and I flew (almost) into Yeppoon. However, it is just one of the new viruses going about and he should be home next week.

Apart from ills we are doing fine and the weather is good. We have had good rain and the pastures are beautiful. I am behind with a lot of work, most of it up-keep like riding and repairing fences, etc. Still, I'll get around to these jobs in time.

While I didn't feel so good, I spent a lot of time in the garden, which sure needed it. The flowers have been lovely. Pansies, balsams, gladiolas, marigolds, lilies, cosmos, etc. Fred and Bigfoot, the only kangaroos we have now, destroyed all the sweet peas. First time I've really been angry with them!

The large flowering trees are all in flower now. The jacarandas are really spectacular, about 30 feet [9 metres] high with light green fern-like foliage and purple bells in clusters. The poinciana tree, about 25 feet [8 metres], is covered in red flowers. Tulip tree, 30 feet, with clusters of large red tulip-shaped blossoms. Indian coral tree, 20 feet [6 metres], with red pea shaped blooms. Cascara with long drooping yellow blossoms. The hibiscus, frangipani and gardenia are just starting to bloom, along with numerous others.

The orchard is looking good too. The grapes are off to a good start and all the citrus trees, oranges, lemons, mandarins, etc. have set new fruit. The tropical apples have just started to bud, along with the avocados, pawpaws, passion fruit and bananas. We had a glorious crop of mulberries this year. Do you have these same trees and fruits in the USA, Fran?

I am mailing a Christmas parcel to you on Monday. However, it will not reach you before Christmas as I read in the paper a couple of days ago that the last surface mail ship to the USA left on 28th October. I'm sorry, Fran, but I just didn't have the parcel ready to send. Anyway I do hope you find everything okay when it reaches you.

Must be off now and home to feed my animals.

Love,

Dulcie

29th January 1975

Dear Fran,

Guess it seems childish to eagerly unwrap a parcel and withdraw all the little packets inside. If we are childish then we certainly enjoy being so. Your package arrived on 5th January and I wish you could have seen us. Len lit up a smoke and lit one of the Eve cigarettes for me and we sat back enjoying these while Terry unwrapped the items. After we had eaten the goodies we did the jigsaw puzzle, had a cup of coffee and another smoke. Wonderful! Thank you, Fran, very much.

Your letter, telling us about the sugar shortage, was very upsetting. Sugar here is regarded as the cheapest item one can buy and is 48 cents for a 2 kg pack (Australia has gone Metric Mad). When I go to Yeppoon tomorrow, I shall inquire about the freight on so many kilograms and see if I can send you some.

Foodstuffs are plentiful here but shortages occur in all motor and machinery parts, tyres and tools. Cigarettes and tobacco are hard to get.

Unemployment is rising fast too, since a great many farmers, cattle growers, etc. have had to walk off their properties and apply for unemployment relief.

It seems so stupid that the government cannot put a maximum on the retailers' profits. Most city folks think the producers are reaping a fortune, but if one cares to find out the facts, it is the "middle man" or distributors and retailers who are making the money. Only now that Australia's farming and cattle, wheat, wool, etc producers are leaving the land has the Government found where the trouble lies.

However nothing has been done and although foodstuffs are plentiful, but expensive at the moment, things must grow progressively worse in the future. Cattle here are worth $5 (five) dollars each in the sales yard at Rockhampton. These beasts cut approximately 450 to 500 pounds [204 to 227 kg] of beef, returning 1 cent a pound to the producers and yet beef still retails in shops from 53 cents a pound for sausages and $2 a pound for steak. [1 pound is nearly half a kilogram.] Since freight to the sales yard is $2.20 per beast, plus yard fees and commission, we end up with 23 cents each for bullocks we have taken 3 years to grow! Does this seem fair?

The neighbours on our eastern boundary, a hardworking German couple who came here some years ago, are farmers, growing vegetables and fruit with irrigation. They receive 5 cents for a cabbage which is sold in the supermarket for 77 cents. Two cents a pound for beans which are 63 cents a pound in the shop. Ten cents a dozen for oranges and these same oranges are retailed in the shop at 11 cents each!

Now the final crunch has come as the farmers, etc. give up producing and draw unemployment relief. And since it is illegal to leave stock unattended, many have shot and destroyed their entire herd of cattle, poultry, sheep and their vegetables and fruit.

Some of our near neighbours and friends have shot 250 head of cattle each week (mainly calves, old cows, bullocks and bulls) and with bulldozers have buried the bodies and will continue to do so until they destroy their entire herd.

With millions of people in the world starving, and our own people out of work and unable to buy the high-priced beef in the shops, this beats me. Senseless, isn't it! And when all the things have been destroyed, what is the population going to survive on?

We are really quite well off since Len still has a job and we are keeping our cattle. We kill our own beef and swap a beast's carcass with the neighbours for vegetables they produce for themselves, since it is not profitable for them to produce for market. So both families are kept in meat and vegetables. My orchard yields us plenty of fruit.

There are certain things we will have to do without. TV for one. The fuel to run the power plant will have to be used sparingly and I shall miss TV at night. Even though the movies were 25 years old, it was company. Especially since Terry started work on 20th January (his birthday). He went with Len as a Cadet Plant Operator. He decided not to go on with school after his Junior Pass as he earns $120 per week as a cadet. After 2 years he earns the same as Len's $11000 a year.

They come home once a month, as Len did last year, and meanwhile I have the house to myself. I'm quite used to working alone all day but the nights seem strange without Terry. Still the neighbours, Gunter and Gertrude Schwartz (the German couple), are only 4 miles [6 km] away and over the years we have taught each other German and English so we can visit and make ourselves understood.

Then I can visit my parents and brother and his wife. They live 8 miles [13 km] from here. Mum and Dad came last night and we had tea together. It is a bit difficult for them since petrol is scarce and so expensive. Although it is slower I find it cheaper to ride a horse when I visit but Mum can't ride.

Well, Fran, it is now 10 pm and I must stoke up the smoke-house before bed. I have a sheep's carcass curing and smoking and ½ pig I've cured and smoking also. Makes delicious bacon.

Love to all,
Dulcie

———✳———✳———✳———

15th March 1975

Dear Fran,

Today is really a beautiful day. Not too hot or cold, just 86 degrees [30 °C], fine with a light breeze. Really, I suppose it is not good weather for rain and it is rather worrying to know that we have had no wet season this year. So far we have had only 6 inches [15 cm] in January and 7 and ½ [19 cm] in February. Nothing this month. By now we should have about 40 inches [102 cm] to carry through to storms in November. However, there is plenty of water and feed as yet and we can only hope another drought is not coming this year. Guess that is something to shelve for the moment.

Worries and unhappy times are always with us, Fran. Guess our ancestors had to cope with problems, too, and so will the future generation and theirs.

Forgive me for pushing advice, Fran, but I do, with the hope that I could help you when you feel that life is like that song "Is that all there is?" Allow me to stand on my "Soapbox" for a while, Fran.

Unhappiness, loneliness, boredom, these seem to be words that so many people use these days to describe their lives. I wonder, is it because men and women drive themselves too hard, thinking only of the material things they can buy? New car, furniture, house, etc. just because others have them, even though the old ones would have been in good working order?

When these new items have been purchased, they find no time to enjoy them as they must go on working for yet another, so there is no time to relax, no time to even do nothing! So unhappiness, boredom and loneliness sets in because there's no time to just waste talking to or playing with one's partner.

In recent years, women have been brain-washed into thinking that they must work at an outside job. That they become cabbages and are useless if they just stay at home caring for the family. This is terribly wrong, Fran. There is a great deal a woman can do at home. Husbands and children never do get around to telling us that we are important. But we should, ourselves, remember that we are the most important (thing?) or person. Just go away for a few days and see what happens!

Naturally without two pay-packets we shall have to do without that new fridge, carpet or whatever the neighbours have. But a poor (perhaps that's not the right word, can't think of another, but you know what I mean) home has love, happiness and Mum there at the end of the day. This way Mum is not worn out from coping with 2 jobs. Her husband is not worn out because he hasn't had to work overtime or worry about extra money for new possessions. And the kids are not lonely and bewildered because Mum is not home from work yet.

Think back to your childhood, Fran, were you happy? Were your parents happy? If so why? If not why? My parents were very poor but we were all happy. Len's parents were slightly better off. This property was more productive, due to the hard work of them both, but they were not happy and parted years ago.

Asking for the honest opinions of Terry and Len, as to if we are all happy and content with life, we all agreed wholeheartedly. Yes!

We have had sad and heartbreaking times, the deaths of Karen and Brendan really rocked us. Then there are floods, fires, droughts, etc. and one watches a lifetime's work fall to pieces, and works 24 hours around the clock to try and save something.

Years ago when we first bought this land, we had an old, half-paid for car and a few pieces of used furniture bought from cane-cutting money. The house we built slowly and the hard way with our own hands. Since we couldn't afford to pay for hired help, both of us built the fences, miles and miles and miles of them. Len always did (and still does) the heavy digging for the post holes with a crow bar while I did the shovelling. The stock-yards, sheds, etc. we built together.

When we ran out of money we went back to cane-cutting, or to fruit picking, anything to get money to build up with. Finally when Terry reached school age, I had to stay here where school services were available. By this time I had learned so much from Len that I was able to repair anything that broke, even the machinery, and take care of the stock, etc. Len was pleased and proud that I became so useful and this helped to save money for other things too.

As time went by and we became better off (about 1969-70) I asked Len if he could stay home instead of working away. He did that year and we managed to get by. However, I could tell he wasn't totally happy and the following year, when we needed money to carry on, because of drought and fire, he went to work doing truck driving at St. Lawrence (200 miles away) [322 km].

It was only then that I realised he needed male company. With just me and Terry for company, Len wasn't happy. So we reached a compromise. He has his job with his mates all week, and drives home Friday nights, returning to work Sunday afternoon. He has a nice caravan, only small, 18 feet [5.5 metres], and sometimes I drive up Saturday morning and return Sunday morning. This is because I can't leave my animals, etc. for too long.

Just as Len can't live constantly here, neither could I leave. I love everything we have built, the garden and my pets and the cattle. Len wouldn't dream of selling, neither would I, as we both agree we shall retire here in our old age.

People often remark that I must be lonely. Others say they envy me my freedom. I'm not lonely, Fran, far from it. I have so much to do and enjoy and I know it's only 5 days before I'll see Len and Terry. When we meet there is so much to talk about. We don't work, just drop everything so we can talk! As to those who envy my freedom, nothing is free, Fran, except that I replace money (that evil thing) with work.

For an example of my days, this morning out of bed at 5:30 am as usual, light the stove (the stove is combustion, burns wood) get the cows, milk, feed dogs, cats, wallabies, kangaroos, etc, etc. Breakfast at 8 am, wash dishes, do floors, beds, etc. Put new exhaust system on car, change 2 tyres, cart molasses for cattle, pump water, bring back load of wood (which I've cut with the chainsaw).

At 3:30 pm, have cup of tea and sandwich. Unload wood, cut it up for stove, sharpen chainsaw. Mow part of the lawn, feed dogs, cats, wallabies, kangaroos, ducks, etc again. Put calves in pen for the night (otherwise no milk in the morning). Fuel, oil and water for light plant. Start engine. Do washing, some ironing from yesterday. Made myself a new dress, pretty, light, cotton voile, for summer. It is 10:30 pm now and I'll leave the hemming and hand sewing for tomorrow night. My dinner is cooking now. Vegetables that the neighbours swapped me for meat I killed yesterday, a good beast that weighed 500 pounds [227 kg], dressed and is tender too.

So most of my entertainment doesn't cost money, Fran, and I am happy and so are Len and Terry.

If I don't feel ready for bed after the work is done, Fran, I make beer, wine, in fact all our drinks are homemade, can't afford anything else. Preserve fruits from our trees and make jam, chutney and bottle surplus vegetables, etc. Knit or crochet pullovers or anything else we need. All these things save money, Fran, and keep me busy. I really find them interesting and a challenge.

As to anyone envying me, then I wonder if they would envy my worn-out floor coverings, covered in muddy dog prints, cat paws, kangaroo feet with big tail drags, etc. Remembering that we have no electricity, just the engine plant which cannot run the stove, refrigerator, iron or anything that draws more than 5 amps. Therefore the freezer, iron and everything else must burn kerosene in small tanks they are equipped with. These things are cantankerous and I've often done my block.

Then there is the heavy chainsaw to fell trees for fire-wood and the stupid old blunt axe to cut it with. Life is not easy Fran, but it is what we make it and whatever we find happiness in doing.

Please come to our poor half-(still!)-completed home for a holiday. I would love to have you, but I think you would be terribly disappointed since we really do live in poverty. But there is no boredom and our home overflows with love and happiness.

Sorry to rave on, Fran, and now I'll step off my soapbox.

Believe me I hope my letter helps you, Fran.

I'll think of you till I hear from you to see if you feel better.

Lots of love, Fran.

Dulcie

———✗———✗———✗———

6th April 1975

Dear Fran,

It is Sunday night and after a hectic but fun weekend, I'm left alone and so have peace in which to answer your letter, which I received on Friday. I am so glad you feel better now. I guess our ways of life are so far apart.

I think watching TV is the greatest thing! That is when the engine is running and when I get the time. I REALLY love the wildlife programmes. Sometimes from South Africa, USA and even Australian programmes. Colour TV has just been introduced into Australia. However we can't afford a set at $900 and anyway we are too far from the transmitters to receive it.

Will you excuse my writing tonight, Fran, it is hard to see. The fuel truck didn't call Friday, as was arranged, and I'm right out of diesel, so I'm using a kerosene lamp. Do you know the kind, a silk mantle is fitted, filled with kerosene pumped up and lit? Gives a small light with lots of shadow (Maybe I need new contact lenses!)

Terry with his motorbike

Len and Terry came home Friday night and brought one of Terry's mates with them. Terry bought a 350cc Honda motorbike for $1100. Since he cannot get a licence till January next year, Len carried it home in his old station wagon and Terry and his friend, David, (who also has a motorbike) rode around and around all weekend. The noise was terrible!

Len's old Holden SW is done. The engine needs new rings and bearings so he left it home today and took my old Valiant. I'll fix the Holden for him so he can take it back next time. Both boys left their bikes here when they went back with Len. (Maybe I'll try to ride a motorbike!)

On the way home Len found 2 dead wallabies (hit by cars). He always stops to see if they have babies and these two did so two new babies for me!

Then on Saturday a stranger came out with another one he had found. He said he had been told that I'd take them. (Good heavens! I'm known as an animal parent or something.) So now I have three new babies to care for. They need feeds every 4 hours, just like human babies, and a waste of time I suppose.

Still I couldn't kill them so I rear them, and those that I can't find good homes for I keep to run about the garden. My garden looks a wreck just now, although last week I did a bit of work in it and planted sweet peas, pansies, larkspurs, cosmos, dianthus and red salvia.

In the vegetable garden I planted turnips, lettuce, tomatoes, cucumbers, beans and corn. (Yummy I love corn!) Love the lot really, people, animals, flowers, plants of all kinds. Len always says that my heart rules my head!

How is your little cat, Fran? He reminds me of one we had, Ginger. He died of old age (10 years) some years ago. The pictures you sent of yours are really nice. He is delightful.

Well, Fran, the light is getting the best of me so I think I'll go to bed.

Do write soon and all my love and best wishes,

Dulcie

6th May 1975

Dear Fran,

Just a note to thank you for the birthday greetings. Catching up to 40 now! Good news on my birthday. Terry has been transferred to the Livingstone Shire Council (our own Shire) so he lives at home again and rides his bike to and from Yeppoon each day. As he is too young for a driver's licence, he has been granted a provisional licence, just to ride from home to work and back.

His bike carries larger plates with P on them and he must be off the road between the hours of 6 pm and 6 am. He is very pleased to be able to transport himself.

Well, Fran, Dad is calling to take me to town so I must hurry.

Best wishes and love,

Dulcie

29th May 1975

Dear Fran,

Today is a disgusting day, cloudy, bleak and cold. Southern states weather that doesn't belong here. I hope it clears off to where it belongs tomorrow.

Today is also Len's birthday. He will be home tomorrow night so I have a cake, etc. waiting for him. Terry is still riding off to work every morning.

Just a thought Fran, what time does work start in USA? Terry leaves here at 6:30 am but work doesn't start until 7:00 am. He finishes at 4:00 pm. Naturally one can't travel in working time so he must leave home in time to be at the job at 7 am. He enjoys his work.

I've a heavy cold at the moment. It must be bugging me a bit because I find I'm rather hot-tempered. The Holden needs engine repairs and, although I have the engine out where I can get at it, I've become annoyed at it for the last 2 days. So I walked off and left it!

The Australian Government has brought in a National Health Scheme. It starts on July 1st. Previously we had a choice of paying doctors and hospital fees or taking out health insurance which cost us $130 per year for man and wife (children over 16 are $65 each extra).

The new scheme means free doctors, consultations and hospital fees, provided one is satisfied with a public ward. This means there are large wards full of people (men, women and children are separated of course) with every type of illness. There is quite a divided opinion on the matter.

As yet we don't know if those who can afford it, and wish to, can carry on with insurance for private treatment. Or if we must all accept the National Health Scheme. It is a very good idea for it means anyone, no matter how poor, can now afford medical treatment and hospitalisation. A great amount of people will now be relieved of suffering and early death.

Still there should be provision made for people to keep insurance for private treatment, if they desire it, as public wards are not always easy to adjust to. With beds spaced 3 feet [91 cm] apart and some snoring, coughing, talking etc. all night, rest would not be easy.

I killed 3 wethers yesterday. I wish I could send you some meat but, like sending sugar, it is impossible. We have been hit with a type of duty or tariff on sending foodstuffs overseas. On 48 pounds [22 kg] of sugar, the duty is $4.80 and the postage $9.20. Plus the sugar cost of $5. This brings the package to $19 for 48 pounds of sugar. Nearly 40 cents per pound [1 pound = 0.45 kg].

What is the world coming to when we can't send food to people? Guess the manufacturers' agents have everything tied up to make a fortune for themselves. Last week I bought 10 ounces of MJB coffee, imported from the USA. The cost was $2.87. I shall certainly be making it last.

Among the vegetables I swapped with the neighbours yesterday, for meat, were beautiful big, crisp, green cucumbers. So this morning I pickled some and from the other vegetables, cauliflower, beans, carrots, etc. I made jars of mixed pickles and relish. The rest I put into the freezer. The perfect day to work in the kitchen! So lovely and warm in here.

My mum has a new kitten. Her old cat died last year. It was ancient and she was very upset over its death. Dad gave her time to get over it a little and bought her a little silver Persian, the same as the old cat. Mum named him Peter (funny name for a cat) and thinks the world of him. I tell her he is not as beautiful as Sugarplum, just to get her biting!

How is your little cat, Fran? His picture always reminds me of the old cat I had before Sugarplum. He was a marmalade cat I named Ginger. Such a friendly old cat. He loved everyone and even strangers could pick him up and he would purr in delight.

But Sugarplum is a one-person cat. I can do anything with him but he bites (never scratches) other people, even Len and Terry, if they put a hand on him. I think I told you before that he is just a wild cat. Terry found him as a kitten after a bush fire. His eyes weren't even open and I had to keep him alive by feeding him with a medicine dropper.

Now he is such a jealous old fellow and still very much a wild cat. He weighs 31 pounds [14 kg], much more than a domesticated cat, and has teeth as long as a dog's. In fact he is bigger than Augy (my dog). His favourite place is on the doorstep and he growls just like a dog at anyone who calls. Should they touch him or me he sinks his teeth into their legs.

Len never liked him because he always glares at Len through slit eyes if he sits near me and has often bitten him. Still Len admits the old devil is a good watchdog (or cat?) so both of them have called a truce and keep their distance. All our friends know him now and don't have any trouble with him providing they do not stand or sit near my chair in the kitchen or lounge. Still, although I love the old devil, I'd like a friendly old cat like Ginger again.

Well, Fran, apart from my old animals, I don't have much to write about. It's just that I hope a few pages of nothing and a couple of pictures every couple of weeks have helped you overcome the depression you were going through a few weeks ago. Do you feel better now, Fran? I do hope so.

Your boys, like Terry, are grown up now and yet they are so precious aren't they? Rick looks so handsome. Is he as serious as the picture shows? No, Fran, Terry doesn't miss school. He loves his work and the bike he bought with the money that he had earned. The whole price of $1200 he worked for and saved (he had to as one must be 21 here to buy on-time payment) and is so proud that it was his effort and not his parents who paid for it.

Terry said to tell Rick his Dodge sounds great and wishes they could swap rides. By now I guess Mark has his licence and I trust he drives carefully. We have seen some TV reports of USA and the traffic is really thick so I understand motorbikes would not be the best thing to drive there.

USA has a pretty fast speed limit compared to us. Maybe this is the cause of so many road deaths, Fran? Still, at a limit of 50 mph [80 kph] on the highways we average about 223 road deaths per year in Queensland and that is too many.

When you consider the population of Australia is 14 million people, and 1204 of them were killed on the roads last year, that's a lot of people.

The law here, Fran, regarding a driver's licence is, if a person lives more than 5 miles [8 km] from a town (or city) hall centre, they can obtain a licence at 18 years of age. If their residence is less than 5 miles from the centre they must be 19 years of age.

If under the age of 18, but over 16, and more than 5 miles distant, they can obtain a P plate permit to drive to work only. (This doesn't give them the right to drive for pleasure or to school, etc.) If they are less than 5 miles then they have to walk or ride a push bike until they are 19. Saves a lot of young lives I think.

Yes Fran, my baby wallabies survived and are now hopping around the garden with the others. A Brisbane zoo took 4 of the grown up ones last week. The agent called and we crated them in dark cages and they were transported by plane to Brisbane. I hope they are happy there.

Well, Fran, I must be going to do some more work. Hope you and family are well.

Love,
Dulcie

27th August 1975

Dear Fran,

It's been a few weeks since I've "talked on paper" as my little niece calls it. You have appeared to be so much happier in your last couple of letters, telling us about Rick's car, etc.

It's wonderful to see you involved with the boys and Dick again, maybe you always were, but I just missed any mention of them in your letters and thought you were feeling left out and depressed. I guess there's always so much we would like to write about but can never think of at the time.

The present economic state of our countries doesn't help us to be cheerful does it? Unemployment is the highest ever, higher than what was called the Great Depression in the 1930s. One person in every 15 is out of work in Australia now.

The primary producers receive so little for their produce that it is not worth carting to market and the townspeople are almost starving. It's so terrible to see people without food when we have it going to waste in the country area. But if I get a semi-trailer to take a load of cattle to the market it costs $11.20 per head and when they are sold we get $5 per head so it just doesn't pay to take foodstuffs to market.

Many people out of work in the towns cannot pay rent or board and are being evicted into the streets. Country people are fortunate, I suppose, in that they at least own their land and homes. And since we have no town electricity supply, or water, or garbage rates, we can get by. We can eat our produce and go without power and use a horse if we have no money to buy fuel.

Terry is out of work and home. Len so far still has his job. Terry gets unemployment relief payments of $36 per week as all unemployed people do. Having our own beef and orchard, and neighbours to swap with for vegetables, along with worn out machinery and cars and a half-built house, we are not mortgaged or in debt. Haven't got much but we will survive

Some of Terry's mates are out of work, with motorbikes to pay off on their unemployment payments. Their parents can't afford to keep them and if they have to pay rent or board they can't meet their bike payments.

We have an old house on our property, it is a big, 60 feet by 53 feet [18 x 16 metres], with verandas all round. It's old, cold and we have been using it to store old garbage, etc. But the boys needed a home so we spent last week cleaning it out, putting a new chimney on the stove and donated our spare Christmas fridge. We got some new mattresses for the old beds and scrubbed out the old cupboards and the boys settled in happily 2 weeks ago.

Strangely enough there's no power plant (they use a kerosene lamp) which means no TV, etc. and the stove is an old type that burns wood and smokes like mad and the fridge (like ours) runs on kerosene. Still they are happy to have a rent-free roof over their heads and they only have to buy kerosene and food.

Terry, of course, lives at home but the houses are only ¼ mile [402 metres] apart so they visit and the other boys are so helpful. They help me with anything I want and I can have plenty of rest because they are learning fast how to kill and skin and cut up a beast.

They are such happy kids, honest, sober and willing to work, but can't get jobs. At least they are safe and cosy and don't have to wander about the towns.

Terry and his mates talked me into buying a motorbike, a small one, 200cc. They told me it would be more economical than the car and faster then a horse but they didn't tell me about riding it! My bones must be made of rubber, Fran, the falls I've had! Riding along cattle pads and into washouts. Oh! Up a steep hill, miss the gears, stall, fall over again! Must be a good bike, nothing has broken yet!

It certainly is cheaper to run than the car, etc. and faster than a horse but oh! my skinned and bruised body. Guess I'll just stick with it till I master it. My parents say it is more expensive to them because they worry about me riding it. They phone home after I've left their house to see if I made it! They didn't do this when I rode a horse over.

Anyway, next time I write, I might be a champion bike rider (Ha Ha).

Lots of love, Fran,
Dulcie

⸻ ✳ ⸻ ✳ ⸻ ✳ ⸻

15th December 1975

Dear Fran,

Not far to Christmas now and Len will be home in just one week's time, hopefully for good, but I really don't think so. Through a lot of political wrangling and eventually with the Queen's assent, Federal Parliament was dissolved and the people went to the polls yesterday for the third time in three years.

Now the new Prime Minister [Malcolm Fraser] has announced it will take three years to correct Australia's economy. So I guess Len will still be going away to work after Christmas. Suppose it's not bad really, at least he has a job when thousands of others are out of work.

Terry is still out of work and draws unemployment ($36 per week).

PS Terry asks how much it is in the USA.

Thankfully, we are not in debt and can grow enough to keep alive, along with Terry's mates who are here and not in debt either. They are good kids, take work when they can find it and come back here to the old house when they are off work.

They are all having Christmas day with us and have already helped me to kill a pig and smoke-cure it. They killed and dressed the fowls and turkeys yesterday and have them all wrapped in the freezer. What wonderful young people! Usually I do this myself but now I'm becoming lazy!

They all rode off on their motorbikes tonight to attend a young friend's wedding. Gosh! They looked so different. Instead of leather jackets, etc, neat suits and tie!

One of the windmills broke on Sunday and the cattle were out of water today in that paddock. The boys helped me rig an emergency pump on the bore today and wanted to watch it tonight, instead of going to the wedding, but I couldn't allow that. So off they went and here am I writing this in the truck while I watch the pump and engine.

Really, I suppose I like it! May seem strange to you, Fran, when you live in a city full of people, and love it, but I like this. Faint moonlight, night bird calls, soft cattle calls, and just the pump engine beat. It's really nice to sit here and watch the cattle, horses and wild animals come to water.

I wish young Rick and his girl every happiness, Fran, but they are so young, aren't they? My married life has been happy but if I had my life over, I would never marry at 17 again. Perhaps it's just longing for something we have never had and would not like when we got it. But still, hard to say, they may live happily ever after, like Cinderella. I do hope so.

I'm glad Mark is going on to school. Terry is not sorry he quit, neither are his friends. The only reason they could give was that they were sick of the routine and study (sorry the light is poor Fran) and being treated as a child by the tutors and having no freedom to live their own life.

Have things altered so much since our days at school, Fran? Were we so stupid that we took whatever was doled out to us? And are we any worse or better off than the young people of today? Wonder if our grandmothers had this to think about?

Hope your parcel arrives in time for Christmas, Fran. I do hope you all have the very best Christmas and the happiest of New Years.

Have a good time, Fran. I will have to close before my battery gets too low.

Merry Christmas and love from,
Dulcie

Friday 13th February 1976 (My lucky day!)

Dear Fran,

What a day to write a letter. Maybe the post office will catch fire or something. Your package arrived, Fran, and as usual Terry tried all the eats first! My choice is the lovely box with the coins. Terry got fussy and wouldn't wear the white hat (he only wears his old cowboy hat) so Len happily went off with it. Guess he looks a picture, driving a dirty greasy old grader along the road with a white hat on! Thank you so much for everything, Fran.

The American Recipe book has some rather unusual dishes. One I tried, Pot Roast Brisket. We all voted it delicious. Strange that in Australia brisket has always been used for dog food with the occasional bit being corned. Our dogs didn't get the last lot from the beast we killed. Just shows how wasteful we are with meat out here. Even though prices in the shops are high, no one tries to use the "off-cuts".

One thing has us puzzled Fran, what is a Dutch oven? [Cast-iron cooking pot with tight-fitting lid.]

The coins are really a treasure. Did I ever tell you Len and I have been collecting coins since we were kids? We have most Australian coins since 1913 (a few older and some overseas ones). The only US ones are from you.

The little booklets (Ford Times) are interesting and I've just been reading about the Everglades.

This is exactly like our coastal area. We go there in the FWD [four-wheel drive] and then crawl on our hands and knees through yucky thick muck and dig out big crabs. Most weigh about 6 pounds [3 kg] and are really nice.

Sometimes we carry a net (the new monofilament net is very light compared to the old linen one) and drag for fish and prawns. Do you call them shrimps?

But we can't drive the last mile or so and the net and other gear gets heavy. There's mossies [mosquitos] and sandflies by the million but no crocs [crocodiles] to eat us. Only sharks and the deadly stone fish. Plus multitudes of snakes that all crawl off in a hurry, thank goodness.

Terry and I took our motorbikes up in the back of the FWD last Sunday and we rode the bikes the last bit. We caught 28 crabs and 500 pounds [227 kg] of mullet (fish), about 4 pounds [2 kg] each. Then we couldn't carry it all back in one trip so we had to ride to and fro in the mud, getting it all back to the Land Rover. The freezers arc all stocked up with delicious seafood but gosh, we earned it, especially me. I kept falling over in the mud and couldn't hold the bike up. Must be a good bike to put up with me. Funny thing, it always starts, even after it's been on its ribs in the mud.

Terry got a job at last, for a few weeks anyway. He helps the curator at the Yeppoon Golf Club, mows, gardens, etc. and it will probably last until the beginning of Autumn, May 1st. Nothing grows much through autumn or winter, not even grass, so I guess he wouldn't get back on till October 30th. Anyway, he likes it and rides the bike in and out.

He leaves home at 6 am and returns at 4 pm so there's 3 hours of daylight left to play about. The wet season is with us, of course, but as yet we have had only 16 inches [40 cm] of rain for the year, so the roads are still all open. It is most unusual weather. Yesterday and today have been fine and hot, 100 [38 °C] yesterday and 102 [39°C] today.

Well, Fran, I must close and start some ironing (my pet hate) so do write soon.

Love,

Dulcie

———✳———✳———✳——

16th June 1976

Dear Fran,

Just a note to send you some of the shots we took on our 5-day show-week holiday. Len and Terry elected to stay home and mind the pets, etc. while Tom, Coral, Irene and Dad went to Shoalwater Bay in the Rover. I went first on the motorbike (so they could pick me up when they found me in the mud!). Mum had her brother staying with her so she did not go either.

The shot from the mountain on Dad's place, Terry took when he and some of his mates rode and climbed it for fun. Gives a rather good picture of the country and I've tried to map it out for you. We camped at the bay and had a good time. Tom climbed Army Mu. with some army fellows and took the shot looking back towards our place. (Love the shot of me and my dad!)

[Unfortunately, these photos are lost and Terry and the family have doubts about the Shoalwater Bay location. However, Terry says, "The whole family used to go fishing and camping at a place called Fishing Creek north of Yeppoon. Dad's uncle owned the surrounding area and we had a great time, and I still have a laugh when I think of my grandfather who never would wear shoes and would stand on the only cactus in the camp area."]

Since then Tom has launched his boat so we may be able to fish in style now. In the paper cutting the name is spelled wrongly. It should be Corene, named for Coral and Irene. Tom is standing beside the mast. Coral's brother, Ray, is walking along the side and our cousin, Tom Holland, was cut out of the picture. Brother Tom worked on it in his spare time. It is made of marine ply, coated all over with fiberglass, which stops barnacles or wood worms or something.

Haven't heard from you since the wedding, Fran. Do hope everything went well and trust they will find the happiness that we have. Perhaps it is harder these days. The young ones need money to buy happiness, I feel, or is it that things are so bad that there is nothing free anymore?

Our fishing trip was so wonderful, cost nothing more than fuel to get there. We camped on the beach, cooked on the coals and the only tracks on the beach were our Rover's and our own feet. But I guess this is something we take for granted. In so many countries there is not the space and quite often people want too many facilities and of course these cost money.

Well, Fran, I am having problems here watching an engine that is a bit "sick" pump water, trying to write while a joey wallaby crawls over me wanting its bottle. Must away and finish today as Terry will be going to Yeppoon on his way to work tomorrow and will post this for me.

Love to all,
Dulcie

—✳︎———✳︎———✳︎—

27th August 1976

Dear Fran,

Happy birthday. Sorry I've been so long answering your June letter. Thank you so much for the wedding photos. They do look lovely. The bride is very attractive.

Funny thing, I was watching a John Denver show on TV the other night. Rick reminds me of him. The film was probably ancient for it to be televised here. It was called John Denver Rocky Mountain High. The scenes of the countryside were so beautiful. Guess we've been led to believe that USA was just a country of big cities but this film just showed how wrong that idea is. Would I be right in saying the Rocky Mountains are in Colorado? If so, there is a whole lot of lovely space there. Strange thing though, there weren't any animals roaming about. Maybe the TV crews scared them.

Winter has been long, dry and the coldest for 7 years. For the first time in my life the temp has been 32 F [0°C] inside the kitchen, even with the fire burning all night. (7 years, I'd say more like 70!) My garden is an utter wreck. Poor old trees are not used to such frost and it will take a while for them to recover.

These pictures I took in May and hoped to follow up with some winter flowering ones. But they've had it. Still, if they recover enough for spring, I'll send some more. About the amount of land we have Fran, only 15,000 acres [6070 hectares] plus the 500-acres [202 hectares] VFL land we took up on a 909 year lease. It is a forestry reserve and one day I hope to have it proclaimed a national park.

I've had a cold for a month or more but it's starting to clear off now. Marvellous things for anyone who wants to lose weight! Speaking of weight Fran, you always said you were overweight. But in the wedding pic you looked really beautiful. Just right and your gown I really adore. Fits and folds beautifully. What type of material is it, Fran? Whatever type you should use it often for clothes as it suits you to a "T".

Well, I must close Fran. Our tax returns should have been

completed on June 30th and I haven't even started them yet. Applied for an exemption to 30th August so I'll be making a mad dash at them for 3 days.

Do write soon, and love,
Dulcie

10th March 1977

Dear Fran,

Forgive me for not writing before. We did receive your parcel and enjoyed the eats, reading and the lovely booze! (Most of all the pretty commemorative plate.)

We had been following the winter US scene on TV. It was really awful. We kept watching for scenes of Michigan but didn't see any. Just as well or I would have imagined I'd seen you in every picture.

The world's weather is crazy for some reason. We had a lousy summer, with bad storms all through and, worst of all, the cyclones. One came while Len and Terry were holidaying about Christmas. One in February and the most recent 5 days ago.

As one neighbour said, he felt like leaving here and telling the world this must be the worst place to live. It is heart-breaking.

During the last two cyclones, Len had gone back to work and Terry wasn't able to get home because of flooded creeks. I never mind being alone but the wind howled and it rained and this last one left 14 inches [36 cm] overnight. Part of the roof of the house blew off and everything got wet. Even the beds were saturated.

When daylight came there was a mess of smashed trees in the garden, roofing iron, and my animals were trying to shelter under the house with 18 inches [46 cm] of water running beneath. Poor little things looked like water rats when I rescued them. But two wallabies were dead.

Sheds were battered and flooded and stores ruined. Fences are wrecked. I've been repairing them and rounding up cattle.

The power plant engine is wrecked. Water poured through the

machinery shed and the engine's fly wheel whipped up the water and threw it into the air-cleaner and alternator. Burnt out the alternator and broke the crank shaft of the engine. Haven't got to fixing that yet. Guess it's not really important and I still have a kerosene lamp.

Terry crossed the creeks on his trail bike yesterday. Haven't seen or heard of him since the cyclone. He brought two loaves of bread with him, wrapped in plastic bags. I could have cried with joy. Funny, I don't know if it was because I knew Terry was okay or if it was because of the bread.

The telephones are still out. They were out for three weeks after the last cyclone so I guess we won't be able to phone anywhere for a while yet.

With due respect to motorbikes, they can be replaced by horses when roads are boggy and trees are blown down everywhere. Poor old "Nightmare" carried me around to see if relatives and friends were all okay. Sometimes we would meet others along the track coming to see if I was okay.

But riding to Yeppoon is a two-day trip for a horse. Now Terry is back, he can collect the mail and news, etc. as he goes to work.

The rain has eased to a drizzle today so we hope for some fine weather. We will sure need it to clean up and repair. Maybe I'm getting old but I feel like throwing the lot.

Maybe I'll fix the light-plant later. Marvellous what light will do to cheer one up. This old kerosine light is about ¼ candle power and I can't see with it anyway. I don't know why I waste a match lighting it.

Terry has the right idea, he jumps into bed and listens to his trannie [transistor radio].

Ah Fran, I'll write again when things are better.

Lots of love,

Dulcie

20th July 1977

Dear Fran,

As usual I'm way behind time with a letter. Thank you for remembering my birthday! Yikes, it is a long time since I've written to you.

Winter has been quite severe this time. The coldest has been 1°C (forgotten what 1 degree would equal in the old Fahrenheit) but there's been more frost than I've seen for about 7 or 8 years.

Water is a problem at the house this time. The cattle bores and dams are holding out good though. Strange how these things take it in turns. So now I'm carting water for domestic supply. At least it is not as much as the stock would take.

Have finished Terry's income tax and almost through Len's and mine. I really hate tax, or maybe not so much the work itself, but staying inside to do the boring stuff.

Terry, June 1977

My garden looks a real wreck. The lawn and a lot of shrubs and trees are frosted black. Some look like dead sticks and a flower is hard to find. Except inside where I have some beautiful Cattleya Orchids in full bloom. I moved the pots into the living room before the coldest nights set in and they have done really well. Maybe they like human company.

Division 3 of the Shire, which includes us, have been trying to get town electricity. We have had a number of meetings with the power authorities and now we seem to be agreeable at last! Power will cost us $10,500 cash for a line to our property and a guarantee of $558 each year for 30 years. I'm not too sure if Len or I will be here that long but the guarantee applies to the property (not the owners). And if it is sold or left to anyone after we have gone, this price still goes on until 30 years are up.

It is a bit expensive but our engine has about had it and a new one will cost $7000. They have a life of about 15 years before they become as unreliable as the old one we have now. It is not working again and I've got tired of fixing it! I've had a week of breaking things, my chainsaw, the Valiant, one motorbike - I wonder what's next?

Anyway I'll have to go and do a bit more work. I have a panel of yard to repair that a bull smashed last week. And then a bullock to get in for killing tomorrow as we are out of beef.

Trust you are all well and write soon.

Love,

Dulcie

Postcard

Happy Birthday

Dreadful business, Dick being ill. He must slow down with the work and go fishing more often. Less work means less money of course but you'll manage, Fran. Marvellous how you coped with everything without Dick and the worry as well. Do hope everything is well now.

Winter is about over thank goodness. The nights are still cold but the days are lovely, 88 [31 °C] today. Yippee, warm at last! Even the trees are sprouting leaves but it is dry, very dry, and there's been some fires about. All fire breaks are done so I hope we will be okay. Getting the garden beds prepared. I must have flowers and vegetables.

Well, Fran, have to go. Do let me know how Dick is and hope everything is fine.

Love,

Dulcie

—✗——✗——✗—

25th October 1977

Dear Fran,

Just a hurried letter but so pleased to know that Dick is much better.

Your summer is over and ours has just started. In Queensland we actually have only two seasons, winter and summer. This year is extremely dry, after the heavy winter. Surprisingly though, water is holding out well but the pasture is scarce.

Since cattle are not worth the freight to market, I'm not feeding them this time. I just shoot those that are too thin to make it through. Mostly cows with baby calves. Better to shoot both before the mother dies and leaves the calf for dingos to kill.

I have been very busy taking all the engines from the bores and dams and putting up [wind]mills. Have 4 up and one to go. Gee, they look good spinning in the wind and pumping water. They will save a tremendous amount of time. No more driving around starting (and fixing!) dirty old diesel engines.

The mills pump continuously with the wind and cost nothing to run. Have just finished putting one on our house water supply and have water running all over the garden and lawn.

My garden looks beautiful, flowers of all kinds and colours everywhere.

Will be a great saving in the long term. No fuel, no repairs, no time wasted on engines. Beats me why we ever went off windmills.

[Photo of garden showing windmill]

The mills cost $1900 each but last for approximately 30 years before repairs to the heads are needed. Guess I won't be climbing up them then. Guess I've had some great muscle building exercises, climbing up and down 4 towers, all 25 feet [7.6 metres] high, for weeks! Dad helped a lot with anything at ground level, but he is a bit too old to climb like a monkey.

Sometimes, when up at the top of the towers, with a strong wind blowing and trying to bolt on the fans, I wished I had a tail. Apart from having a clean up without engines, we also got rid of our old cars.

Len bought a Falcon and I bought another Holden. I traded my old Valiant and Len gave his old Holden to Terry for a shooting bomb. First thing Terry did was to tear off the doors and knock out the windscreen so he could shoot straight through! Looks terrific!

Now I'll have lots of spare time to do things I've always wanted to do. Maybe I'll start to finish the house first. That is after I've got my vegetable garden finished.

Did I tell you before that the German people who used to swap veggies for beef, no longer grow much as the husband had a heart attack and is receiving a pension now. They are very nice people and I still supply them with beef. But I can't expect the old lady to grow veggies for me. She is not well either.

I must ask, Fran, if you have already sent a Christmas parcel. If not, I wonder do you think we might pass them up now? The postage is so high it's hardly worth it anymore. Maybe sometimes I might find something really worthwhile to send over to you but unless it's really one good item then I don't think I'll make it every Christmas.

If you would like me to continue our usual parcel, please say so, Fran. But with Dick not so well I wonder should we be extravagant for this year, anyway. Please don't be hurt about my suggestion, Fran. Let me know your wishes.

Well, I must go as Terry will be home soon, looking for something to eat.

Lots of love, and hope everything is well in your corner of the world.

Dulcie

13th December 1977

Dear Fran,

Good to hear from you again. Wish I could send you some of our lovely warm weather. Watched a Saturday report on TV last night. Cleveland, Ohio, buried in snow and the wind was blowing people over on the streets. Gee, I hate winter but our winters are not that bad! Amazing how anyone or animals, birds and such, survive.

Does the cold kill people at all, Fran? Summer has settled in well here. Around 100 [38°C] most days but cools off to mid 70's [25°C] at night. We've had some good storms. The first couple brought 7 inches [18 cm] of rain and I just about cried with joy. The grass is all lovely and green again and what's left of the cattle, etc. can at last have full stomachs.

Len brought my brother Brian's twins down last weekend. They are staying for Christmas. They are 12 now and Tom's little girl, Irene, is 5 and ½. Tom and Coral live only a few miles [3km] away so I'm teaching the twins to ride the little 175cc trail bike so they can double over for visits.

Since Brian moved to town with them, at the age of 3, they haven't had any chance to drive or ride and are really quite dumb when it comes to doing anything here. It's unheard of for a child any older than 8 not to be capable of driving a tractor, car, or anything else in this part of the country. Still they are learning fast after a few "wipe outs".

We are planning a pre-Christmas barbecue about the 21st, since Len doesn't come home till then, and we always have a Christmas tree too! But I don't bother with an inside one, we just trim one of the pine trees growing outside. Only trouble is, every year they get higher and higher and this year I don't think we will have the star on top.

I planted 3 new ones last year, thinking we would use them, but the boys insist on the larger one. Glad it's the young ones who climb the ladder!

Well, Fran, I must away. Merry Christmas to you all and a very happy New Year.

Love,
Dulcie

20th February 1978

Dear Fran,

Someone's taken off with all the writing paper so this will just have to be brief.

You sure have been tucking into the goodies! Gadding about to restaurants, I really envy you.

Last Sunday and we killed and cut up and I went with Mum and Dad to a hotel. (Wonder if I should tell Len!) The hotels are allowed to open from 4 pm to 6 pm and such a hot day as well. We enjoyed a cold beer and bought a ticket in a raffle. Guess what! I won and wouldn't you just know it the prize was a tray of steak. Yuk! After cutting meat up all day!

We had 19 inches [48 cm] of rain 2 weeks ago and now it's so hot you can hardly find a mud-hole anywhere and just last week I got bogged!

Terry turned 19 the same day as Rick's birthday. The last of his teen years. Did I tell you he passed his exams and is now a qualified green-keeper? But I've got the worst looking lawn in the district! Even worse since yesterday. A couple of the horses got in and stamped all over it, making great hoof holes and chewed patches.

The rain perked up my garden. The zinnias are a picture and the vegetable plot is doing well. Have cucumber, pumpkin, beetroot, carrot, lettuce and tomatoes. Will put in some cabbage today. The fruit trees are loaded this year. Hope we don't get a cyclone this time. February-March is the cyclone season so we are keeping our fingers crossed.

Well, Fran, I must away and post this and head for home. Best wishes and happiness when you move into your new home. Sounds lovely.

Love,
Dulcie

3rd July 1978

Dear Fran,

Good to hear from you again and many thanks for the birthday card. I love the azaleas on the card. Wish mine would grow and flower like that. Guess it's too hot here for them, they don't do well. Have been about 1 foot [30 cm] high for years and get a few flowers on sometimes.

It's good Dick got away from his business. I hope he gets something easier, close to your new lake home. Maybe he's like me.

If I lived by a lake I wouldn't do any work, just fish all day long and probably starve to death!

Trust you had a wow of a time for your parent's Golden Wedding anniversary. Wish them many more happy years from us, Fran. If Len's parents were still living together they would be married for 53 years now. Guess they can't celebrate it, can they? Len's dad hasn't been too well lately. He had a couple of heart attacks this year. But he is 83 so I guess it's to be expected.

We've had a good winter so far, just a couple of light frosts and some welcome rain. Hope you are enjoying spring. I always remember a twig of soft furry things you sent once. Pussy Tails I think you called them. My twig lasted for ages but everyone kept feeling it and finally the little furry things fell apart.

I have a new baby wallaby, a little black one. He is cute. Hops around the house and makes puddles where he shouldn't. Whatever became of your Punk and the stray female cat you found, Fran?

[Fran says that 'Punk' was short for her orange cat 'Pumpkin' and the stray female cat was Mary Kat which turned out to be a male cat - not discovered for several more years.]

Old Sugarplum is still going strong, He is 11 now, fatter than ever and weighs 36 pounds [16 kg] and shames that vet who said he was overweight 3 years ago and wouldn't live long. His only exercise is walking from his feed bowl to his chair and back, and a daily trip outside to his burial ground. What a life, and us humans are told to eat less and exercise more!

Income tax time is around for us again and I'll have to settle into a session of return forms for Terry and us. Will be a bit more complicated this year as we have both new vehicles and machinery. Did I tell you in April that we bought a new light-plant, direct-coupled to a 240 volt alternator? Was I glad to get the old one carted away. Dirty old hard-to-start, unreliable thing!

I'm also trying to transfer my half of the property over to Terry so that Len and Terry will be joint owners. Bit difficult, as we have gift duties in Queensland, and the property has to be valued and duties assessed. Could be too much for us to manage. Latest assessment value is $150,000 and duties payable to government,

$10,000. Can't get out of it unless I die and leave it to him and I sure don't feel sick yet.

I don't mean I'm clearing out, Fran. Just that I'd like to see Terry own it now as it isn't much good, him doing work here, weekends, etc. and investing his money in (rather than spending his money on) doing and building things on the property, when he can't receive anything out of it.

Seems rather a stupid law that children have to wait until their parents (or one of them) are dead. After all, Terry might be 70 years old before we die! Len was 50 three weeks before my 41st birthday, and as Len said, he is half-way to 100! Hope he makes it.

Well, Fran, must off now as I have some mending and ironing to do before bedtime.

Trust all is well with you and yours.

Love,

Dulcie

PS Write soon.

7th September 1978

Dear Fran,

Your new home looks lovely. The snow really looks nice. I've never seen snow but winter just ended here so guess I don't really want to see snow! I'm glad Dick and you are happy there and hope you have many happy years beside the lake. Tell Dick to send me a picture of the "big ones" he catches.

Fran, your cat is almost as bad as Sugarplum! Wish they could meet each other. Two fat pigs aren't they? Your boys, like Terry, are men now. I love Mark's beard. We see the odd beard and long hair on Southern tourists but they didn't catch on much up here. Too hot I suppose.

Rain is falling lightly today so I'm having the afternoon at home. I killed yesterday evening and cut the carcass up, packed it, and froze it this morning. Was a good beast, not over-fat, and weighed out well.

Fran, your idea of selling the land to Terry cheap is basically what people try to do to avoid gift duty. But that is where the trouble starts now because the law prohibits the sale or transfer of land, or any property for that matter, between husband-wife-children without government valuation.

One way around it would be to sell the land at $1 per hectare to a friend and then the friend could sell it to Terry for the same. This has been done in some cases and once the friend gets hold of it you find out the friend isn't a friend! So it's better to do it the costly way and be sure. However we haven't had much time to go on with it lately.

Len's father was staying with me for 6 weeks through winter. Len's sister, Margaret, takes him sometimes but she has 6 children and hasn't been too well lately. Anyway, Len came home for the weekend while his dad was here and he went back to his job on Sunday at about 2 o'clock (13th August).

Pop went to bed early as usual and at 5:30 next morning I took him a cup of tea but he was dead. He had passed away through the night in his sleep. Problems and problems after I telephoned the ambulance who came and pronounced him dead. They will not carry dead people so I called the police. Interviews and statements for 2 hours. They have to be sure it's not a case of murder, one said! A man of 83, what next?

Then they called the police van and took Pop to the morgue. I phoned Margaret, that's easy, but can only get Len on the 2-way radio and he turns it off mostly after the 7 am call. He is 327 miles [526 km] from here, all gravel road and a long trip, so I didn't want to go looking for him unless I had to. Called the sign every half hour until another man, who works with Len but 42 miles [68 km] apart, answered.

He drove to Len and passed the message on at 11:45 am. Len got home that night. He had left here on Sunday, 15 hours before his father died, and it took 7 more hours to contact him and another

6-hour drive for him to come home. After the funeral, 2 days later, more problems.

Pop was a Catholic, so is Margaret and his deceased daughter's children. He was buried from his own church and I cried for Len. Because, of his 7 grandsons, Terry, who Pop referred to as his only non-Catholic grandchild, was the only one of his grandsons who went to his funeral. And he was a pall-bearer along with Len, my brother Tom, my own old dad, Len's cousin and one friend.

Then to cap it all he left his entire estate to Len's mother whom he had parted from approximately 25 years ago. Now Margaret is contesting the will because the parents were separated and Mother is a non-Catholic. Oh goodness, what a lot of trouble religion can cause.

Len's opinion is that if his dad left Mother the estate, even though they had been separate for years, then she is certainly entitled to it. So we have no part of it now but I feel for Mother, and the trouble ahead, because I like her too. She has been a good friend to me for years.

Anyway, Fran, somehow I still feel religion can break a family and I'm glad my family, although of mixed faith, are very close.

Lots of love,
Dulcie

24th April 1979

Dear Fran,

So sorry to have taken so long to write, just sheer neglect on my part. Would often think I'd write to you but each time I opened the desk, bills and bookwork would spill out and I'd get side-tracked on them. Other times I just closed it up and forgot the lot!

Last November 20th, Len's sister, Margaret, lost her youngest child, aged 3 and ½, in an accident. She broke up completely and was taken off for mental help. She is still there. They have always been fairly well off, and employ a live-in housekeeper, but she refused to take charge of the other kids so they came to us. Twin boys 12, a girl 11, twin boys (again) 8 and a girl 6. Beds all through the living room and kids everywhere. They sure make loads of work. Wish I could afford a housekeeper! Ah well, maybe Margaret will soon be better and home again to take care of them again.

Christmas was noise and mess and fights and to top it off, Terry was put off at the golf course. Due to the economics of the country, the club went bankrupt and it's no longer open. He couldn't stand the 6 kids and their noise and got another job away from home. He comes home every second Sunday to see how things are. Len, too, has taken to every second weekend. Maybe the dog and cat will clear out next!

[Terry, (left) with a friend, May 1979]

Anyway the summer weather was good and we've had good rain to go into winter with. Cattle prices are slowly coming up again. What spare time I do have is spent on the stock and my garden is quite wrecked. These kids don't know how to use a spade or digging fork and what's more they don't believe they should. Tell me that is the gardener's job and I should employ one! They are fast coming down a peg and learning to do things after school and at weekends.

I'm glad Dick is better and has a job to suit him, Fran, just as long as he doesn't over-do it. I agree with you on the fireplaces, Fran. Most of the older homes here have at least one in the living room. Some even have 2 or 3 in the larger old places. But I feel sorry for those now building as fireplaces have become a thing of the past and one must crouch beside an electric heater.

Well, I have a pile of ironing for school tomorrow so I must off and I will try to write more often.

Love,
Dulcie

20th June 1979

Dear Fran,

Good to hear from you again. Rain is falling today. We have had 45 mm so far. Winter is late this year but after the rain clears I guess the cold will really get started. Always does after rain.

I think your petrol is a bit cheaper than ours. Have enclosed some house listings and used-car prices, also a fuel invoice. Our fuel comes in a bulk tanker and is pumped into our storage tanks but for those who buy from service station pumps it is about 3 or 4 cents a litre dearer. Unleaded petrol is called standard and is 28 cents a litre. About 4 litres to the gallon makes it $1.12 per gallon as we are paying in bulk.

Most people are buying the smaller Japanese cars and the American Fords. Valiants, etc. are slowly disappearing off the roads. Terry and I both have 6-cylinder Holdens and average about 28 miles [45 km] per gallon. Len has a Ford 6 cylinder and gets about 19 [30 km] or at the best 22 miles [35 km]. The difference is the horsepower. Len's big engine isn't really necessary. Granted, the car can go faster but what's the use? Australia's open-road speed limit is

60 miles per hour [97 kph]. Anyway the roads are so crook [bad] you can hardly do that!

Len's sister is home again. Came back 2 weeks ago and the kids all went home yesterday. What a relief! I hope Margaret pulls herself together and gets better. Len is right. He said she wants a good smack, where it will hurt most, and do some work for herself, instead of paying others to do it for her. He thinks she is spoilt and pampered.

Anyway, the kids learned a few things while they were here. Weeds have to be pulled out of the garden and a spade digs the ground before plants are put in. How to make beds and clean floors, etc. In the end they were very willing and eager to try anything. They all want to come back during holidays but one or two at a time is enough!

Well, Fran, I must go and feed my animals before it gets too late. It's still raining so I guess it will be dark early tonight. Seems strange to be alone now, especially now that Terry has gone too. What a small meal I'll have to cook tonight. Write soon.

Lots of love,
Dulcie

10th August 1979

Dear Fran,

Haven't heard from you for a while and I'm not sure if I owe you a letter. Hope you and Dick are both well and still happy with your new home. I guess it must be what you call Fall over there now. Winter is gone here and summer has got off to a good start. Will be soon fire danger time and I had Tom here today replacing the rollers in our dozer tracks so that I can crawl around the fire breaks again.

Tom and Coral gave a surprise party for our Silver Wedding Anniversary on 10th July. (Actually the party was Saturday night 14th.) Was really a surprise as we had spent from daylight to dark, non-stop even for a meal, pulling pipes and the pump out of the 96 bore. Put on a new pump and lowered the lot down again and connected the windmill just on dark. When we got home, Coral phoned to ask us to a party, which we refused until she told us what it was about. We were the last to arrive but it was a very nice night even though we were tired.

Only thing to spoil it was Terry smashed his car up. He had been in on the secret and was driving down from Saraji on Friday night. One cattle property, Annandale, has a habit of running stock out on the road and Terry hit a horse. The owner said he couldn't pay for the damages and Terry has no insurance. He phoned a mate and towed his wreck back. Then his mate brought him down Saturday night. On the way they shot 7 horses and 16 head of cattle, still on the road at Annandale. Since then the Stock Inspector has shot a few more and said he will continue to until the roads are clear of straying stock. Still that doesn't help pay to repair Terry's car, or all the others who have smashed up there during the last year, since this new owner bought the place.

Snoopy has just come in to be picked up. Did I tell you about him before? He is a red wallaby and was born blind. Cooberrie Park Zoo owns his mother and she tossed him out because she sensed something was wrong with him. The zoo people gave the little fellow to me last October because they didn't have time to bother with him. When the children were here the eldest girl always spoilt him and now he still likes to sit on my lap and have a sleep. He is about 2 feet [61 cm] high and weighs 20 pounds [9 kg] now. But when he is full grown will be close to 6 feet [183 cm]. He can walk around the garden and through the house and never bumps into anything unless it is left out of place. Well, Fran, I must off and do a few more chores before dark.

Love,
Dulcie

24th August 1979

Dear Fran,

Guess I'm expecting the impossible, hoping these flowers will reach you in perfect condition. I wanted you to have them when Dick's birthday party is on. I once read that if plants are spoken to they respond. Well, these didn't understand me because I begged them to open last week but the buds just stayed tight and ignored me! Still, I hope you have a wonderful party and happy birthday, Dick, from us.

You and Dick are still spring chickens, Fran. Len was 51 last May and I turned 42 last April. It's not a bad age, past all the baby days and school and worries about what the future has in store for the youngsters. Feels good now that we have our homes and everything else we need and free of debt.

Remember 20 years ago, worrying about how to pay your way along? Mortgage, car payment, school books, etc. At our Silver Wedding party someone asked us if we had any regrets. At the time we said no but later at home we both had a thought for the two little ones we lost so long ago. Two small regrettable parts of our lives.

It's impossible to describe just how their deaths knocked the bottom out of our world, which we saw, as all young ones do, through rose-coloured glasses. But we had each other and most of all Terry. It's been great to have him at home for so long.

When he first moved away to Saraji, the quiet nights used to haunt me. But now I know that he is a young man and must leave the nest, like a young bird.

Len takes his long service leave next February so I'll have him home for a few months, which will put old Sugarplum's nose out of joint! Living alone, I quite often talk to him and he laps up the attention! Poor old fellow will be 12 years old in September. He is still as fat as ever, 32 pounds [14.5 kg], and still has a beautiful set of teeth that he sometimes uses on my leg if he wants feeding and I'm a bit late.

I think without all my animals around the place I would have gone batty or taken to drink years ago. But when the day's work is done it's wonderful to come home and walk around the garden and say hello to all the pets. Most relaxing.

Well, Fran, must relax off to bed. As I said before, have a wonderful night for Dick's party and I'll keep my fingers crossed for the flowers.

Love,
Dulcie

5th October 1979

Dear Fran,

While rounding up cattle the other day, these wild orchids reminded me of the exotic flowers I sent. These wild ones grow all over the trees. There are other types but I couldn't reach them. The cattle and horses pull them down and I've noticed the blooms on the ground for over a week so maybe these will get to you in a fair condition. They are not very pretty but still hope you can see a bit of our country if they arrive okay.

I agree it was a big step for you to change homes and jobs. Good luck to you. I do hope everything works out well for you both. I guess I'm too "stuck in the mud" to move now. Really, I know I couldn't, so that's why all buyers' offers are refused. I can't really explain why but any amount of money couldn't shift me now.

I love the country, where we have put so much work into, and I love my animals and know they wouldn't settle if moved elsewhere. And Terry, who will own the property when we are gone, plans to keep it for his lifetime and his children (if he has any).

Talking of children, we are all excited. A new baby is to come to the family again. Tom and Coral expect a baby in March. Irene is 7 and ½ now and Coral had been to so many specialists and was always told she would never have any more. So we have been throwing our hats in the air and already celebrating the event. Terry's comment, "Gee, mum, when it's as old as I am, I'll be as old as you." Poor old Terry.

Well, Fran, I must off and feed my pets and wrap up the flowers for you. Not being close to town, one has to search for something to wrap with and my good Parker is dry and this lousy old 20-cent Bic doesn't write when it should. Still I want you to have just a small part of our world, in case I'm not here to do it again, (getting old you know).

Lots of love,
Dulcie

Tuesday 27th November 1979

Dear Fran,

For once I envy you enjoying the cold weather! Has been a little too hot for comfort lately. Seems a widespread heat-wave over most of central Queensland, with temp readings of 47°C in the shade, about 115 on the old Fahrenheit scale. No rain and the grass is burning off fast, not to mention the water evaporation. Really hope it rains soon or we will be in trouble with the stock.

I drove up to Rockhampton yesterday to inspect a Caterpillar bulldozer we wanted to buy. Seemed like 147 [64°C] in the city and I was glad to get home to some shady trees. Coral went too, to do some shopping, and you know how long it takes to inspect machinery and test it. And the day wore on.

When I picked Coral up, the poor girl had about had it. Being pregnant in the heat is not comfortable. Anyway, the machine had too much wear in the pins and bushes, idlers and rollers, for the price they were asking, $26,000. Wouldn't drop the price so I didn't take it. Back again and I had to start the light-plant.

Yes, Fran, $900 air fare to USA does seem reasonable, but still money and time are not easy to find and I think the fare is dearer when it's summer in the USA. Perhaps we Aussies would die in the American winter!

Lending rates on money here is 11½% but there is a way to dodge that. For instance we have money invested in the ANZ Bank and receive 12% interest. We can draw it at any time if we want to. But we can leave it there to earn 12% and borrow the same amount at 2% interest.

Complicated, but for instance if we had $20,000 invested and received 2½% per cent per annum and we wanted to borrow $20,000 then we still receive 12% on our money and pay only 2% on the borrowed money, so we earn 10% clear still. We have convinced Terry it is wise to invest his money, too, at the bank. There are other "get rich quick" investment companies that pay higher interest, but the bank seems safer.

Terry boards all week at his job, and comes home weekends, so I'm still alone, Fran. It doesn't worry me now as I'm used to it. Oh yes, I bought a new piano a couple of weeks ago. The old one was rather seedy so now I amuse myself at night and time passes quickly to bedtime.

I wonder what's going to happen to the US hostages in Iran? Why isn't the Shah sent back as the Iran students demand? Why doesn't President Carter drop a bomb on Iran? Perhaps we are not told the true reason why the Shah is in the USA. Perhaps he is not ill, just hiding. Would he be taking millions of dollars to USA and so the government wants him and are willing to sacrifice the hostages? Do you think Kennedy will defeat Carter, Fran?

Guess I'll have to leave this. A bulb blew sometime back so I'll have to fix it before I begin to write sideways.

Back again and now I can see the page. Lightning is flicking miles off to the west so maybe a storm for someone. Hope rain falls for them and a little comes our way by morning. Nights are so hot and sticky with moths and bugs crawling about the lights.

One of my possums just followed me in and is sitting on the desk eating an apple. Funny little bright-eyed furry things. Guess I'd better take her out soon and close the screen door. So hope you are all well and write soon, Fran. Let me know how Kentucky was.

Love,
Dulcie

—✳— —✳— —✳—

30th January 1980

Dear Fran,

Eleven months left in the "new" year and are we having a long heatwave! From November to now the days are well into the 100s [38°C]. Plenty of dry electrical storms. In fact, a 19-year-old mate of Terry's was struck by lightning last week. He was mustering cattle and how many times have we told the young ones to get off their horses and leave them. Lightning always seems to be attracted by horses. Anyway, the lad was dead when his father found him.

We had a hot Christmas but enjoyed Christmas dinner with all the family and friends coming. We had 32 people to dinner and the sides of the house bulged out.

Terry had a party for his 21st. We were going to have a barbecue but the weather didn't suit so we changed to Lake Serpentine and everyone had a marvellous time. Eats, swimming and games. Terry's cousin, Kim, was 21 two days before and, as his mother's dead and his father doesn't seem to care much about the children since his re-marriage, Kim and Terry's party was combined.

Fortunately, they were on holiday to recover. Us too! Terry and Len are both back at work now. Len helped me with some cattle while he was home and sold 2 semi-loads (60 head). Prices are coming up again, $393 a head. It is thought prices will rise and peak about the last quarter of the year and possibly fall in 1981. So I must send off more about June if we get any rain.

We also found time to do some fishing, first time for years. We have been able to drive the Land Rover there instead of bikes. Sure is dry up that end, but we caught stacks of crabs and some good fish.

The fish are getting smaller though, most around 4 to 5 pounds. [1.8 - 2.2 kg] I think the trawlers off the coast are taking all the good ones. Tom is out in his boat trawling too. I haven't heard from him so he can't have his box full yet. I hope he does well. They need a good few catches to help with costs of the new baby to come.

And the best news is last, Fran. After a meeting, a delegation took various proposals to the Federal Government (bypassing the State Government) and the news was broadcast last week. The Federal Government has stopped the [Japanese] Iwasaki Company from purchasing any more land in Queensland.

And if Iwasaki does not commence to build or develop the property he now has, by March 1980, the Federal Government will reclaim the whole lot. It will therefore be Crown Land and can either be declared a National Reserve or Wild Life Reserve, or it can be sold in equal portions by the Crown at public auction to Australian Citizens. So we haven't lost yet, even though the High Court let us down!

You see Federal Law states that land cannot be owned by one particular person or company for more than 2 years without being developed or used. Not even a block of land in towns to build a home on. This stops the greedy from buying up vast areas or blocks and holding them to make profits. The last we heard, the State Government Premier had no comment to make. For once he is beaten!

Oh well, best go and feed my animals and do a few jobs before my bones grow together.

Lots of love,
Dulcie

—*—*—*—

28th May 1980

Dear Fran,

Your country is certainly getting a beating. I see on TV films of Mount Saint Helen's volcano and earth tremors in San Francisco.

I read many years ago a story about San Francisco but don't know if it is true. Was stated that holes had been drilled and tested, plus lots of other things and, to cut a long story short, San Francisco would one day be demolished by earthquake. Let's hope it doesn't happen. I never knew the USA had any active volcanos either. Australia supposedly doesn't.

I trust your horrible snow has gone and you are enjoying spring. Winter hasn't started here yet, very late this year. But I'm taking no chances and bought a new truck in February and have been busy selling off as many cattle as I can. We didn't get any autumn rain so it could be dry by spring.

Coral had a son (April 10th) and named him Tom III. He is really beautiful but rules his mum. She even moved into the spare room to sleep with him till Tom (his dad) called a halt.

All these Tom's are very confusing. When my brother Tom was young, people used to call dad, Big Tom, and my brother Little Tom. In later years it became Old Tom and Young Tom. Now there's another one!

Terry came home last weekend. He hasn't been home for 8 weeks because it is such a long way. It takes till mid-day Saturday to get here and he has to leave noon Sunday. He looks so grown up now but has been working long hours. He is studying to operate a Water Treatment and Sewage Plant at night and has to spend from 7 pm to 11 pm, three nights a week, at the city water plant.

Yeppoon is supposed to be building a water treatment and sewage plant next year and, if Terry passes his course, he plans on applying for the position of operator. He brought home two little dogs for me.

My old dog, Augy, died in his sleep some weeks ago. Quite upset me when I got out of bed one morning and he was dead on his mat. When Terry phoned one night I told him and he must have thought I needed two to take care of in the house. There are the cattle dogs outside of course but working dogs can't be pampered and spoiled inside because they won't work properly.

Wish you could see the new ones, Fran. One is black and a very friendly little pup. The other is a Silky Terrier, masses of long silky hair and such a funny little face. I don't know if they will ever be as good a mate as Augy but they fill a gap and are good company, especially at night. The black one is named Soot and the little hairy one, Scruffy. Old Sugarplum doesn't care much for them and after a few whacks to their noses, they keep clear of him.

I've been fencing and picking pumpkins today. Have about 2

tons of pumpkins so far, and more for tomorrow, so guess I best get off to bed and rest the muscles!

Write soon and hope you are all well.

Love,

Dulcie

25th July 1980

Dear Fran,

Rain is falling tonight - how lovely - we need it but not as badly as Texas, USA. I see on TV pictures of the drought there. How well I know what it is. I'm sorry for the people and the animals.

How about your printing business? Great! But, Fran, don't overdo the work load. Hey, you and Dick look so young, what's the secret? Gee, Dick is so handsome, wouldn't mind stealing him from you! Be a good idea really. He could print things for me. Recently I had about 40 sheets to be photo-copied and the old machine coughed, wheezed and groaned before it finally turned out the copies. Only last week I completed our taxation return and typing that and a copy was hard enough.

So glad you've had 25 years of marriage. Isn't hard is it? Our 26th came up on July 10th and we bought a dozen orchid plants for the garden. Hope they flower every year.

Terry came back from Brisbane last weekend. Reached home at 4 in the morning. Long drive for the poor kid after sitting for his exams. Ten hours down and ten hours back. Still he thinks he has done fairly well. I hope so.

I went up to Rockhampton last week and bought a new Leyland tractor and plough and the tractor has a blade too. So now I can learn how to use it and off to work. This rain is good. It will soften the soil. This will have to be my last new unit for this year. What with a new truck, chainsaw, etc. I've spent my budget for 1980.

My new dogs, Scruffy and Soot, are coming along very well although old Sugarplum still gives them a paw-full of claws every so often. And Rachel, my kangaroo rat, bites Scruffy every chance she gets. Poor dog turns and runs! Soot can't stand the piano being played and howls horribly. Maybe it's the way I play!

Still miss old Augy though. He was so clever. Knew when I put my good clothes on, he couldn't come because I was going out. If I put on my house shoes and garden hat, I was just pottering in the garden. But if I put on my riding boots, clothes and hat, he always beat me to the gate. But they all have to go some time and at least these two fill a gap. Even though I didn't need two. Well, the rain is still falling and I must off to bed. Do write soon and tell me how your business is going.

Good luck to you both.

Love,

Dulcie

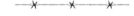

10th December 1980

Dear Fran,

Sorry I've been slack at letter writing. I notice your last letter was in October.

I finally finished all the ploughing and planting. Took ages and ages but now we have had rain and there's hectares of beautiful green fodder. Quite a sight for sore eyes. I'm glad the crop is up and away before the wet season starts in a few weeks. Shouldn't have any erosion problems.

The inland areas have been badly affected by drought and the rabbits have travelled to the coast. I dug a burrow out last week and found 7 baby rabbits. They are so cute, little furry things about the size of kittens. Couldn't resist keeping them.

I don't expect the rabbits to be much of a pest because they won't have much hope of survival here. Once the wet sets in they will all drown in their burrows or be washed away. Scruffy dog is afraid of the little ones. They try to cuddle up to him and he races off and hides!

Terry was home for 2 weeks holiday. He left Utah Coal Company and moved to Middlemount. He won't be home for Christmas as they haven't got an assistant qualified to relieve him yet.

[Middlemount was a coal company town built almost overnight for coal workers and opened by the Duke of Edinburgh.]

He bought a new car while he was home and brought his girl to stay too and was very helpful doing some of the ploughing, etc. The girl, not being a country girl, found things a bit different, but was very good, prepared meals, etc. for when we came home.

She wants to learn to drive but did Terry have to start teaching her with the semi-truck? Poor girl was terrified and she said she only wanted to drive a car. But Terry said driving is driving and that means everything and she should be grateful he took the stock trailer off the prime mover!

I can see Terry will have to change his mind about what girls are capable of doing or he will be an old bachelor.

When I was in hospital, in August, my black dog died, so I didn't get another one as Scruffy is a big enough pest. He is about 7 inches high and won't grow any bigger but he can't wait to go outside the garden fence and boss the cattle dogs around. But he runs away from baby rabbits.

Sugarplum ignores him so when he's out at the barns he clashes with all the farm cats and gets quite a few scratches. Old Sugarplum is hardly able to walk now. He limps badly and just gets about.

The vet examined him but there's nothing can be done. He has arthritis in the leg joints.

Well, I have the last load of cattle to truck to the sale yards tomorrow morning (last for 1980) and won't be selling anymore until the wet is over so I'll be able to have a spell and do a bit of gardening.

Do have a Merry Christmas and Happy New Year.

Lots of love,

Dulcie

Card
9th May 1981

Your kind expression of sympathy is gratefully acknowledged and deeply appreciated from the family of the late Dulcie Clarke 21-4-37—30-3-81.

Terry

F GLObKe
9691 BLaCKFOOL Court
Coldwater MI.49036

U . S . A

Your kind expression
of sympathy
is gratefully acknowledged
and deeply appreciated
From the family oF
the Late DULCIE
CLARKE
ZI-4-37 · 30-3-81

terry.

16th May 1981

Dear Terry,

I was deeply saddened upon hearing from you about your mother. It was a great shock! I had always dreamed of someday meeting with her in person.

As you know our friendship began over half our lifetime ago

when we were both newly married young girls. Through the years we shared many parts of our life, many happy and many sad.

Throughout I always had a deep admiration of Dulcie. Her sweet singing, her compassion and love for the animals she tended, her openheartedness at taking care of people who needed help; her love for nature and your property. But the one trait I always admired the most was her courage. She always met life head on. No task was too big for her, nor too hard. She saw what had to be done and she did it, like to or not!

I shall miss her too. And someday if you could, please write and tell me what happened and tell me how you are doing too. And please remember if you ever come to the US you know I would love to have you spend some time here with us.

As ever,
Fran.

———✳——✳——✳——

EPILOGUE

Truth is truly stranger than fiction.
Fran Globke, 2021

One can only imagine Fran's shock, back in 1981, when she received the sympathy card from Terry, announcing his mother's death. There was no warning or explanation.

The card, so short and so abrupt, presumed that Fran had already been informed of Dulcie's death by either Terry or Len. I asked Fran when, and how, she had been notified of Dulcie's death.

She replied:

The last letter [from Dulcie] was in December 1980. The next correspondence was the thank you/sympathy card from Terry that I am enclosing, listing date of death as March 30, 1981. I wrote him but neither he nor Len ever answered.

Joe and I stared at the writing on the forty-year-old card, trying to guess what had happened.

Why had Dulcie passed away?

Why hadn't Len or Terry replied to Fran?

Why was Terry's handwriting so strange?

Why did my research find no record of the death of a Dulcie Clarke in 1981?

It even occurred to me that Terry might have been illiterate and unable to write back. Of course, we soon ruled out that ridiculous theory. If Terry hadn't written that card then perhaps it was Len?

Fran's letter to Terry was never answered and for the next forty years she continued to miss and grieve for her friend. She kept all Dulcie's letters safe and often thought about her lost soulmate.

One day, she promised herself, *I'll do something with these letters. They are too precious to lose and they are important historical documents.*

Time passed.

Fast forward forty years to November 2020 when Fran's email from Michigan, US, landed in my inbox. I was captivated before I had even reached the end of it.

Joe and I became involved. We promised Fran that, if we could, we would transcribe and publish Dulcie's letters and share them with the world.

The project engrossed us and Dulcie's story both enchanted and shocked us. But, like Fran, we found it hard to accept Dulcie's sudden and unexplained death. It was all too odd and left us feeling uneasy and dissatisfied.

Strangely, it was the image of a long-dead kangaroo that eventually helped us solve the mystery. Although I hadn't yet found any trace of Dulcie on the internet, she had left plenty of clues in her letters to Fran. Clarke with an 'e'. Bungundarra. The towns of Yeppoon and Rockhampton. The names Terry and Len.

I searched through Facebook without much hope. It was possible that neither Terry nor Len were still alive, or they didn't use Facebook.

I found a young man in Queensland named Adam Clarke but he was much too young. Idly I scrolled down his timeline and then stopped. My heart skipped a beat. I stared at a black and white photo Adam had posted up some months ago.

The caption read: *Grandma with a huge roo.*

Somehow, I absolutely *knew* I was looking at Dulcie. Was it possible that Adam could be the grandson of Len and Dulcie?

It took me a full 24 hours before I reached out to Adam, partly because I didn't want to be disappointed and neither did I want to disappoint Fran.

With Joe at my elbow, I took a deep breath and sent Adam a private Facebook message.

The conversation went like this:

ME: *Hi Adam, apologies for contacting you as a complete stranger. My name is Victoria and I have a really random question about a pic on your timeline. Was your Grandma's name Dulcie by any chance?*

ADAM: *Yes, that was her name. How do you know her? She passed away last June.*

You could have heard a pin drop. Joe and I gaped at each other. We'd found Dulcie! But she'd passed away in June 2020? How could that be? Did we not have the right Dulcie after all? I didn't know how to answer. My fingers refused to type. Long pause.

ADAM: *Hi, I'd like to know how you knew my grandma. It's amazing you picked her from that photo.*

ME: *Hi Adam, thanks so much for your reply. Sadly, I didn't know your grandma. Sorry to be so mysterious, but I just wanted to check that I have the right family. Would you mind telling me the name of Dulcie's husband, or your father, or the place where they used to live?*

ADAM: *Are you doing a family history? There's a lot of things that I only just found out. Dulcie's husband (my grandad) is known locally as Len but his name is Tom Clarke. They had a farm at Bungundarra outside of Yeppoon, Queensland.*

Joe and I gasped. We'd found Dulcie! My reply did not convey how excited we were.

ME: *Thanks for that, it sounds like I have the right family.*

ADAM: *I'm very curious now.*

ME: *One last question, is your dad still alive? Sorry to ask.*

ADAM: *Yeah, he's still going strong.*

ME: *Oh, good!*

ADAM: *I'm still interested to know where this is going.*

ME: *I am an author and also have a small publishing company that specialises in publishing books about people's lives. Recently one of my readers contacted me saying she had some letters in her safekeeping from a penpal in Australia who died a long time ago and wondered whether I would like to publish them in a book. The letters are about day-to-day life running a farm.*

ADAM: *So the letters are my grandma's?*

ME: *Yes, I think so, but they ended suddenly in 1981 when her penpal was informed that Dulcie died. That's why I'm so surprised you said she died last June.*

ADAM: *Well, if you send a photo of her writing, it's very distinct. This is getting weirder.*

ME: *So strange. I don't have the original handwritten letters but I do have a snippet. I'll find it and take a screenshot.*

ADAM: *Yeah that would be great. Be good to see.*

ME: *Here it is, found it.*

ADAM: *Looks like her writing. If you have the address too, it must be her.*

ME: *No question, we have the right family.*

ADAM: *We didn't know of her writing letters.*

ME: *Dulcie mentioned receiving parcels for the family from Fran, the penpal. They included toys for Terry, your dad. Perhaps he can shed some light on those times.*

ADAM: *My dad is on Facebook. You can contact him. It would be a good book. True hard times. Have a talk with him.*

ME: *Will do. Thanks so much for your help, really grateful.*

I immediately contacted Terry. (Oh, the wonders of modern technology!)

ME: *Hello Terry, please excuse me for bothering you, but I've been having a long chat with Adam and he suggested I contact you. I am an author and also have a small publishing company that specialises in publishing books about people's lives. Recently one of my readers contacted me saying she had some letters in her safe keeping from a penpal in Australia and wondered whether I would like to publish them. The letters are about day-to-day life running a farm in the 1950s, '60s and '70s and would be interesting for people interested in farm life in those days. We think the letters were written by your mother.*

Several hours passed until, finally, a reply came from Terry.

TERRY: *Hi Victoria, nice to hear from you. I must say that the world is a small place. Who would have thought a photo of my mother that was taken in the early 1950s and is on my son's Facebook page could be noticed by somebody?*

ME: *Hi Terry! How nice of you to get back to me. I had a great chat with Adam today, he was really helpful. I never thought that we'd find your mum's family! Such a lovely surprise.*

TERRY: *If you would like to ring me we can have a chat.*

And so I dialled the number he gave me and we talked for over an hour. Terry was utterly courteous and charming and did not hold back, answering all my many questions and volunteering facts I knew nothing about. An avalanche of fascinating photos landed in my inbox over the following weeks.

I'm sure we both found that first phone call slightly surreal. Terry was describing his mother to an unknown English woman, and I was talking to somebody who I felt I'd known since he was born even though Terry and I are the same age. Through Dulcie's letters, I'd seen him grow from a baby to an adult. I knew when he had cut his teeth, about his childhood illnesses, his school results, his first motorbike and when he left home.

"And what about Len, your father? When did he pass away?" I asked.

"Dad? He's still alive, he's in the next room. He's 91 years old now. "

"And Dulcie didn't pass away in 1981?" I asked again.

"No. Absolutely not," Terry replied.

"And that card Fran received, you didn't send it?"

"Nope, that never happened, I'd already left home. Mum died last June, I'll send you her death certificate."

Terry kindly did send Dulcie's death certificate, leaving us with that same question.

Who had sent that sympathy card?

We can only conclude that Dulcie, herself, had sent it to Fran.

Why? Who knows.

"The land at Bungundarra was all divided up into parcels and expensive properties on acreage were built for weekenders," Terry told me. "My parents sold the farm and divorced in 1989 and Mum became a recluse with very little contact with her grandkids or any other family members. She was 83 when she died in hospital of cancer. When I cleared her house out, I found some old letters from an American in Michigan, but I threw them out. I didn't know who wrote them or that they had any value."

We already knew that his mother had lived an extraordinarily hard life, but Terry explained that she'd also had some ongoing mental issues. Perhaps she just couldn't cope with life, and keeping up a brave face with Fran was too difficult. Perhaps that's why she ended the letter-writing. But she kept Fran's letters until the day she died.

My next email to Fran was hard to write and bitter-sweet. I had so much news. We had found Dulcie's son, Terry, and Dulcie's twin grandsons, Adam and Heath. We had Terry's backing for the book and a heap more photographs.

But I had to tell Fran that Dulcie had faked her own death.

Fran was deeply shocked but stoic. I will let her have the final words in this extraordinary odyssey of love and pain.

I am so glad you wrote me about all of it, she wrote. *I always want to know the truth and not be shielded even though it is done with the best of intentions to protect me. I wonder if we will ever know the whole story.*

I also looked through my journals to see what was happening in my life then. I think both of us were entering a new life style. Empty-nesters almost. I had been through low points and Dulcie helped me with her "soap box" letter in March 1975.

After Dick's illness, we sold our business, and left family and friends to move a 100 miles from Detroit to Coldwater, a small rural community, and bought a lovely house on the lake with no jobs or any real plans. Just to get Dick healthy again. And in 1980 we bought a franchise in a copy/print shop and began our new life. And it seems Dulcie found a new life too, not the death we had thought.

When our youngest son Mark drowned in the lake while home after graduating Magna Cum Laude from College in 82, some of the strength I found to deal with it I am sure can be attributed to how Dulcie had lived her life.

After her "death" I have had a whole different life with great challenges and achievements and happiness I could not have imagined and full of peaks and valleys.

Bungundarra means "hills and hollows" and I am content.
Fran Globke, 2021

A REQUEST...

Authors absolutely rely on readers' reviews. Without them, books don't get noticed.

If you enjoyed this book, we'd be so grateful if you left a review, even if it's simply one sentence.

And if you could recommend this book to your local librarian, we'd be eternally grateful.

It's available in paperback, large print paperback, hardback and large print hardback editions.

THANK YOU!

ACKNOWLEDGEMENTS

I am much indebted to Fran for allowing me to collate Dulcie's letters in a single volume. As the recipient of the letters, she recognised their beauty and historical value and kept them safe for well over half a century. Thanks to her, we have an intimate account of farm life in rural Queensland during the 1950s, '60s and '70s.

My thanks to Dulcie's son, Terry, for allowing me to publish his mother's letters. His unstinting generosity cannot be overstated. Without his support and assistance, this book might never have seen the light of day. He was unsparing in time and effort and provided many of the photographs that illustrate the volume.

My thanks to Dulcie's grandson, Adam, for answering my first message when I started searching for the Clarke family, and the valuable information that he provided about his grandmother.

Grateful thanks to the beta readers of *Dear Fran, Love Dulcie*. Thank you Julie Haigh, Beth Haslam, Elizabeth Moore, Val Poore and Pat Ellis for your time, enthusiasm, and ability to spot errors before the book was launched.

Disclaimer

Both Fran, and Dulcie's son, Terry, have granted me full permission to reproduce Dulcie's letters. However, readers should be aware that surviving family members have stated that Dulcie was given to exaggeration and that some of the events she describes may be inaccurate. Opinions differ, even within the family. I respect the family's views that, over the years, Dulcie may have had issues and "lost herself". I also know from personal experience that memories are subjective. No two people remember the same event in precisely the same way.

It is possible that the letters may be subject to flawed memories, imagination or exaggeration. Nevertheless, I urge the reader to accept the letters at face value in the knowledge that they are exactly as Dulcie wrote them at the time.

Each book purchased will help support Careflight, an Australian aero-medical charity that attends emergencies, however remote.

ABOUT VICTORIA TWEAD

Victoria Twead is the founder of Ant Press which has been involved with publishing memoirs since 2011.

After living in a remote mountain village in Spain for eleven years, and owning probably the most dangerous cockerel in Europe, Victoria and her husband, Joe, retired to Australia where another joyous life-chapter has begun.

Victoria is the New York Times bestselling author of *Chickens, Mules and Two Old Fools* and the subsequent books in the Old Fools series. Her days are now spent adding to the Old Fools series, helping authors publish their own memoirs and playing Princesses with her granddaughters.

Email: TopHen@VictoriaTwead.com (emails welcome)
Website: www.VictoriaTwead.com
Old Fools' updates Signup: www.VictoriaTwead.com
This includes the latest Old Fools' news, free books, book recommendations, and recipe. Guaranteed spam-free and sent out every few months.
Free Stuff: http://www.victoriatwead.com/Free-Stuff/

Facebook: https://www.facebook.com/VictoriaTwead (friend requests welcome)
Instagram: @victoria.twead
Twitter: @VictoriaTwead
Patreon: https://www.patreon.com/VictoriaTwead

We Love Memoirs

Join Victoria and other memoir authors and readers in the We Love Memoirs Facebook group, the friendliest group on Facebook.
www.facebook.com/groups/welovememoirs/

THE OLD FOOLS SERIES

INTERNATIONAL BESTSELLING MEMOIR SERIES FROM
VICTORIA TWEAD

  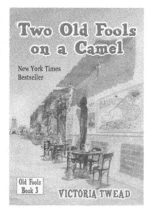

Book #1 **Chickens, Mules and Two Old Fools**
If Joe and Vicky had known what relocating to a tiny Spanish
mountain village would REALLY be like, they might have
hesitated...

Book #2 **Two Old Fools - Olé!**
Vicky and Joe have finished fixing up their house and look forward
to peaceful days enjoying their retirement. Then the fish van arrives,
and instead of delivering fresh fish, disgorges the Ufarte family.

Book #3 **Two Old Fools on a Camel**
Reluctantly, Vicky and Joe leave Spain to work for a year in the
Middle East. Incredibly, the Arab revolution erupted, throwing
them into violent events that made world headlines.
New York Times bestseller three times

 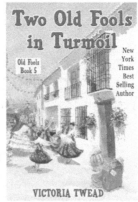 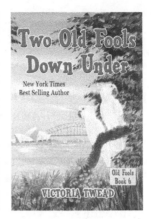

Book #4 **Two Old Fools in Spain Again**
Life refuses to stand still in tiny El Hoyo. Lola Ufarte's behaviour surprises nobody, but when a millionaire becomes a neighbour, the village turns into a battleground.

Book #5 **Two Old Fools in Turmoil**
When dark, sinister clouds loom, Victoria and Joe find themselves facing life-changing decisions. Happily, silver linings also abound. A fresh new face joins the cast of well-known characters but the return of a bad penny may be more than some can handle.

Book #6 **Two Old Fools Down Under**
When Vicky and Joe wave goodbye to their beloved Spanish village, they face their future in Australia with some trepidation. Now they must build a new life amongst strangers, snakes and spiders the size of saucers. Accompanied by their enthusiastic new puppy, Lola, adventures abound, both heartwarming and terrifying.

Two Old Fools in the Kitchen, Part 1 (COOKBOOK)
The *Old Fools' Kitchen* cookbooks were created in response to frequent requests from readers of the *Old Fools series* asking to see all the recipes collected together in one place.

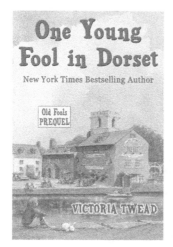 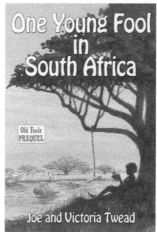

One Young Fool in Dorset (PREQUEL)
This light and charming story is the delightful prequel to Victoria Twead's Old Fools series. Her childhood memories are vividly portrayed, leaving the reader chuckling and enjoying a warm sense of comfortable nostalgia.

One Young Fool in South Africa (PREQUEL)
Who is Joe Twead? What happened before Joe met Victoria and they moved to a crazy Spanish mountain village? Joe vividly paints his childhood memories despite constant heckling from Victoria at his elbow.

ANT PRESS BOOKS
AWESOME AUTHORS ~ AWESOME BOOKS

If you enjoyed this book, you may also enjoy these Ant Press titles:

MEMOIRS

Dear Fran, Love Dulcie: Life and Death in the Hills and Hollows of Bygone Australia collated by Victoria Twead

Chickens, Mules and Two Old Fools by Victoria Twead (Wall Street Journal Top 10 bestseller)
Two Old Fools ~ Olé! by Victoria Twead
Two Old Fools on a Camel by Victoria Twead (thrice New York Times bestseller)
Two Old Fools in Spain Again by Victoria Twead
Two Old Fools in Turmoil by Victoria Twead
Two Old Fools Down Under by Victoria Twead
One Young Fool in Dorset (Prequel) by Victoria Twead
One Young Fool in South Africa (Prequel) by Joe and Victoria Twead
Two Old Fools Boxset, Books 1-3 by Victoria Twead

Fat Dogs and French Estates ~ Part I by Beth Haslam
Fat Dogs and French Estates ~ Part II by Beth Haslam
Fat Dogs and French Estates ~ Part III by Beth Haslam
Fat Dogs and French Estates ~ Part IV by Beth Haslam
Fat Dogs and French Estates ~ Part V by Beth Haslam
Fat Dogs and French Estates ~ Boxset, Parts 1-3 by Beth Haslam

From Moulin Rouge to Gaudi's City by EJ Bauer
From Gaudi's City to Granada's Red Palace by EJ Bauer

South to Barcelona: A New Life in Spain by Vernon Lacey

Simon Ships Out: How One Brave, Stray Cat Became a Worldwide Hero by Jacky Donovan
Smoky: How a Tiny Yorkshire Terrier Became a World War II American Army Hero, Therapy Dog and Hollywood Star by Jacky Donovan
Smart as a Whip: A Madcap Journey of Laughter, Love, Disasters and Triumphs by Jacky Donovan

Heartprints of Africa: A Family's Story of Faith, Love, Adventure, and Turmoil by Cinda Adams Brooks
How not to be a Soldier: My Antics in the British Army by Lorna McCann
Moment of Surrender: My Journey Through Prescription Drug Addiction to Hope and Renewal by Pj Laube

One of its Legs are Both the Same by Mike Cavanagh
A Pocket Full of Days, Part 1 by Mike Cavanagh
A Pocket Full of Days, Part 2 by Mike Cavanagh

Horizon Fever 1: Explorer A E Filby's own account of his extraordinary expedition through Africa, 1931-1935 by A E Filby
Horizon Fever 2: Explorer AE Filby's own account of his extraordinary Australasian Adventures, 1921-1931 by A E Filby

Completely Cats - Stories with Cattitude by Beth Haslam and Zoe Marr

Fresh Eggs and Dog Beds: Living the Dream in Rural Ireland by Nick Albert
Fresh Eggs and Dog Beds 2: Still Living the Dream in Rural Ireland by Nick Albert
Fresh Eggs and Dog Beds 3: More Living the Dream in Rural Ireland by Nick Albert
Fresh Eggs and Dog Beds 4: More Living the Dream in Rural Ireland by Nick Albert

Don't Do It Like This: How NOT to move to Spain by Joe Cawley, Victoria Twead and Alan Parks

Longing for Africa: Journeys Inspired by the Life of Jane Goodall. Part One: Ethiopia by Annie Schrank
Longing for Africa: Journeys Inspired by the Life of Jane Goodall. Part Two: Kenya by Annie Schrank

A Kiss Behind the Castanets: My Love Affair with Spain by Jean Roberts
Life Beyond the Castanets: My Love Affair with Spain by Jean Roberts

The Sunny Side of the Alps: From Scotland to Slovenia on a Shoestring by Roy Clark

FICTION

A is for Abigail by Victoria Twead (Sixpenny Cross 1)
B is for Bella by Victoria Twead (Sixpenny Cross 2)
C is for the Captain by Victoria Twead (Sixpenny Cross 3)
D is for Dexter by Victoria Twead
The Sixpenny Cross Collection, Vols 1-3 by Victoria Twead

NON FICTION

How to Write a Bestselling Memoir by Victoria Twead
Two Old Fools in the Kitchen, Part 1 by Victoria Twead

LARGE PRINT BOOKS

Chickens, Mules and Two Old Fools by Victoria Twead (Wall Street Journal Top 10 bestseller)
Two Old Fools ~ Olé! by Victoria Twead
Two Old Fools on a Camel by Victoria Twead (thrice New York Times bestseller)
Two Old Fools in Spain Again by Victoria Twead
Two Old Fools in Turmoil by Victoria Twead

Two Old Fools Down Under by Victoria Twead
One Young Fool in Dorset (The Prequel) by Victoria Twead
One Young Fool in South Africa (The Prequel) by Joe and Victoria Twead

Fat Dogs and French Estates ~ Part I by Beth Haslam
Fat Dogs and French Estates ~ Part II by Beth Haslam
Fat Dogs and French Estates ~ Part III by Beth Haslam
Fat Dogs and French Estates ~ Part IV by Beth Haslam
Fat Dogs and French Estates ~ Part V by Beth Haslam

A Kiss Behind the Castanets: My Love Affair with Spain by Jean Roberts

Horizon Fever 1: Explorer A E Filby's own account of his extraordinary expedition through Africa, 1931-1935 by A E Filby
Horizon Fever 2: Explorer AE Filby's own account of his extraordinary Australasian Adventures, 1921-1931 by A E Filby

A is for Abigail by Victoria Twead (Sixpenny Cross 1)
B is for Bella by Victoria Twead (Sixpenny Cross 2)
C is for the Captain by Victoria Twead (Sixpenny Cross 3)

How to Write a Bestselling Memoir by Victoria Twead

ANT PRESS ONLINE

Why not check out Ant Press's online presence and follow our social media accounts for news of forthcoming books and special offers?

Website: www.antpress.org
Email: admin@antpress.org
Facebook: www.facebook.com/AntPress
Instagram: www.instagram.com/publishwithantpress
Twitter: www.twitter.com/Ant_Press

HAVE YOU WRITTEN A BOOK?

Would you love to see your book published? Ant Press can help! Take a look at www.antpress.org or contact Victoria directly.

Email: TopHen@VictoriaTwead.com